PENGUIN
BOOKS

Clear English

Vivian Summers was educated at the universities of Exeter and Cambridge. For many years he was the Head of the English Department at a large West Country school and he has lectured at a College of Education and the International Summer Schools of Exeter University. He has written several books on English language and literature and is the author of *Public Speaking* (Penguin, 1988).

Clear English

Vivian Summers

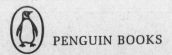
PENGUIN BOOKS

PENGUIN BOOKS

Published by the Penguin Group
Penguin Books Ltd, 27 Wrights Lane, London W8 5TZ, England
Viking Penguin, a division of Penguin Books USA Inc.
375 Hudson Street, New York, New York 10014, USA
Penguin Books Australia Ltd, Ringwood, Victoria, Australia
Penguin Books Canada Ltd, 2801 John Street, Markham, Ontario, Canada L3R 1B4
Penguin Books (NZ) Ltd, 182–190 Wairau Road, Auckland 10, New Zealand

Penguin Books Ltd, Registered Offices: Harmondsworth, Middlesex, England

First published 1991
10 9 8 7 6 5 4 3 2 1

Filmset in Linotron 202 Melior

Printed in England by Clays Ltd, St Ives plc

For Isolde

Contents

Introduction

It sounds the easiest thing in the world to write down clearly and simply what is in your mind. Yet thousands of people are daunted by the prospect of writing even a short business letter in their own language. To write anything longer seems to be quite beyond them. In this book we assume that you are one of these people, lacking in self-confidence when a pen is in your hand and unsure what is correct English and what is not. In your work or social life you feel the need to write but you simply do not know how to go about it. What is worse, you believe you may be prone to mistakes in English expression but are lacking the knowledge that could ensure you avoid them. How do you begin to tackle your problems?

First, let's see what skills you already possess. You may be surprised at your own expertise.

You *speak* English fluently and expressively. You have no difficulty in communicating with others in all the complexities of daily life at home and at work.

You have a large vocabulary of English words already at your disposal.

You frequently create grammatical structures of great complexity: 'When I saw the man who repaired our roof last year I was so angry I could hardly tell him what I thought of him.'

The problem with writing is that it has to be *precise* and *permanent*. When you are expressing yourself in speech, you can say the same thing over and over again in slightly different ways until you are sure the listener understands you correctly. When you have finished, your words have vanished into thin air and no one can go back over them with the absolute certainty that they are recalling exactly what you said (unless a tape recorder has been used).

In writing, your words have to speak for themselves once and for all and they remain on the paper to be read over and over again, always saying the same thing. What is more, you cannot judge by the look on your recipient's face how well you are being understood (as you can with speech). There is no possibility of rephrasing your remarks and trying again. You have to convey your meaning quite precisely at the moment of writing.

This alone is a challenge. But there is a further obstacle to confident writing. This is the need to be 'correct'. However casual and informal our speech, our writing is expected to conform to certain well-established conventions and to show an understanding of the structure of the language. People are very ready to criticize faults in the writings of others even though they may be unable to do better themselves. We are judged by the way we write and, however unfair it may be, an error of spelling or a mistake in grammar will make people condemn us as ignorant and uneducated.

A little background

There are two schools of thought about learning how to write. One says that the skill will be best learned by experiencing 'language in practice' in all its varieties, written and spoken. It believes that mastery of expression is caught rather than taught and that a student who is motivated to write will find the way to do so. The role of the teacher is to provide this varied language experience through books and recordings and by devising situations that will stimulate the student to explore language for himself. The teacher then provides advice and guidance as required. This attitude has been in the forefront of the teaching of English for the last twenty years or more.

An opposing point of view is widely regarded as the old-fashioned one. This sees English as a system obeying rules of grammar and sentence structure which have to be learned in detail and applied rigorously. It seems academically respectable because it makes the study of English similar to that of Latin – for centuries the staple of English education. It also makes the study of English difficult, laborious and, for the majority of pupils, just plain boring. It does not even automatically produce good writing, hence the swing to the freer and less structured approach of the post-war period with its emphasis on 'creative writing' rather than the rules of grammar.

Although the new method had its successes, it was not the complete answer. Students undoubtedly produced more interesting and imaginative pieces of work than under the old system, but they lacked a firm knowledge of the way language works and the security this brings in writing grammatically. Readers are very quick to detect errors in punctuation and lapses in grammar, yet too many students brought up on 'creative' writing are unable to explain when it is correct to use a comma, a semicolon or even a full stop and what makes a sentence a sentence!

In 1988 a government Committee of Inquiry, set up to consider the teaching of English in schools, published its report. This was the *Kingman Report* (named after its chairman, Sir John Kingman) and it decided that a middle course between the rival methods was the answer. It rejected calls for a return to the old-fashioned method of formal grammar teaching and the use of language exercises divorced from the context of the students' experience. But it also declared quite firmly:

> Language is, as a matter of observable fact, plainly governed by a series of conventions related to the various audiences, contexts and purposes of its use.
>
> Successful communication depends upon a recognition and accurate use of these rules and conventions. Command of these rules and conventions is more likely to increase the freedom of the individual than diminish it.

The Kingman Committee also set out the skills in language use which should be expected of children at the ages of seven, eleven and sixteen and the Committee supported the idea of formal testing of children at these ages.

If you are reading this book, it may be because you feel that your own schooling did not give you the confidence in the use of English that you wish you had. You will be interested to know what the Kingman Committee believes a sixteen-year-old should be able to do. The list includes the ability to punctuate according to the conventions of Standard English; spell correctly; use a wide and varied vocabulary appropriate to different contexts; understand and use a variety of sentence structures; use varieties of language which appropriately express different degrees of formality and informality; be able clearly to express feelings as well as facts and arguments. It requires the use of simple technical terms in which to discuss language and there is also a requirement for sixteen-year-olds to speak

Standard English using their own accents and to read aloud effectively.

This list may suggest to you that the old-fashioned mastering of the rules has won the battle over creativity, which has to take second place in the aims of English teaching. This is not necessarily so. The requirement that competent sixteen-year-olds should be able 'clearly to express feelings as well as facts and arguments' shows that the main purpose of creative writing has not been ignored. The remark, quoted earlier, to the effect that the command of rules and conventions is more likely to increase the freedom of the individual to communicate effectively, supports this view. If this book gives considerable space to technical matters – rules and conventions – it does so in the same spirit as the *Kingman Report* and in the belief that having confidence in one's ability to use the tools of the writing trade will enhance the ability of writers to express themselves more adequately and satisfyingly than they would if hampered by ignorance over grammatical rules and uncertainty about how to undertake the craft of writing. The intention of this book is to show you how to overcome some of the obstacles to clear English, to achieve the targets set out above and to enable you to write with a confidence in yourself to say what you mean.

1   To Begin With . . .

There are three elements in every piece of writing: the writer, the reader and the message. Each will affect the way you write.

The writer

This is you of course. But you would be wrong to think that you are the one element that never changes. You will write in one way as the applicant for a job and quite differently as an irate customer complaining about a faulty television set. Your letter to an old friend about a holiday in Spain will be different from the article you write for the local paper and your style will be different again if you are writing a report on the holiday for a market research organization. In each case you are adopting a certain role and the way you write should reflect this. You can imagine how surprised your old friend would be if your letter read like a business report and how unimpressed the editor would be if you submitted a travel article which turned out to be a chatty letter. Very probably you will instinctively adopt the role suitable for a particular piece of writing but it is as well to be clear in your own mind at the start how you see yourself – applicant, complainant, gossiping friend, expert, etc.

The reader

Your aim in writing must be to make an effect of some kind on the person who reads your words. You therefore have to consider your reader very carefully indeed. If you are writing a letter, you will either know your reader personally or (in the case of a business letter) will know his or her place in an organization. This means you should have quite a good idea about the person you are writing to and *what he or she expects from the letter*. This matter of expectation is important. You may surprise and amuse your correspondent by writing in an unusual style, but you are far more likely to cause annoyance or offence. People – especially in business – are quite set in their ways when it comes to correspondence and the wrong style, grammatical errors, mistakes in spelling, will ruin the effect of your letter.

Your piece of writing may be a business report and so your readers will be managers and business colleagues. They will not expect a personal approach but something formal, businesslike, and, above all, clear and to the point. Literary flourishes and personal asides will be quite out of place. The success of this kind of writing depends on your skill in reducing a complicated set of facts and figures to something easily understandable on which important decisions can be based. This is the expectation you have to bear in mind as you write.

What group of people produces the largest amount of writing? The chances are that not even the newspaper industry can exceed the torrent of words poured out every day by students in schools and colleges. Perhaps you are reading this book because you are finding that higher education demands skills in writing that have grown rusty since your schooldays or perhaps you never were 'good at English'. Lecturers and teachers constantly complain that students are unable to express themselves adequately in their assignments and, as a student, *your teacher is the reader* whom you have to consider when you write your assignment. You will know the teacher for whom you are writing – and he or she may have trained you in the style required. If you have not been given this instruction, then you should assume that a formal approach is expected as if you were writing for a general readership. Your work may also be read by external examiners and you have to assume that these readers are experts in the subject who are looking for a clear exposition of your response to their questions. Some examining boards, particularly in subjects where personal opinions and reactions are sought, welcome a fresh and informal approach and will not penalize small inaccuracies of expression. But, unless you are very sure that this style is acceptable, you will be well advised to maintain a formal style and write as accurately as you are able. This may not be easy *if your grasp of the topic is shaky or confused.*

The message

This last point leads us directly to the heart of the matter: *you cannot write clear English if you are not clear in your mind what you want to say.* To put it another way, English expression cannot be divorced from the material you want to convey. You may know all about English grammar, the rules of spelling and punctuation and you may possess an ample vocabulary, but these will not produce clear English if you are uncertain about your subject matter. *Often the act of writing is itself a struggle to bring order to what is a confused and complex set of impressions in the mind.* Many great writers would agree that this has been the origin and motivation of their works. For those of us whose ambitions do not go beyond writing good letters, effective reports or successful essays, the principle still applies: we must work out in our preliminary thinking and as we go about our writing exactly what we want to say. This may involve a few jotted notes, but it will more probably lead us into 'thinking while writing' and then editing and redrafting what we have written until we are certain we have produced the best version of which we are capable. One disadvantage of the traditional examination essay is that it has to be done rapidly and with no chance for redrafting and improvement. But for most of our writings there is time for working on our script to make it as effective as possible. This is something we should expect to do with any important piece of writing.

Summary

Be clear in your own mind about your role as a writer. Think carefully about the expectations of your reader(s). Realize that you cannot write clear English if you are not clear in your mind about what you want to say.

Accept that the very act of writing is part of the process towards clarification of your meaning.

Therefore be prepared to draft and redraft your writing as often as is necessary to produce a satisfactory final version.

2 Tried and Tested: Some Basic Rules

There are some well-tried pieces of advice that often occur in books on the art of writing. We will consider them straight away. Then we can assume that we will be applying them to all the different kinds of writing we shall undertake.

1. Prefer the short sentence to the long

It is very easy, when considering a subject as complex as the art of English, to construct sentences with several clauses and subclauses, phrases and parentheses – even when one is trying to avoid complexity – and in the end confuse the reader instead of enlightening him by producing a sentence as long and tortuous as this one which you are reading! The gist of that ungainly sentence could have been stated more clearly in three short sentences:

> The art of English is a complex subject. When discussing it, one can too easily produce highly complicated sentences. These confuse the reader instead of enlightening him.

2. Choose a simple word where possible

We all know how some people love to use long words in order to impress others with their importance. The 'men from the Ministries' are notorious for this, though in fairness to them we have to admit that the Civil Service has made great efforts in recent years to overcome its former reputation for obscurity and pomposity.

The following short list gives examples of long words and their shorter equivalents:

> Anticipating – awaiting
> Communicate – write

Dispatch – send
Expedite – hasten
Indigenous – native
Initiate – start
Modify – change
Proximity – nearness
Remuneration – pay
Terminate – end

No two words carry exactly the same significance. Even if the basic meaning is the same, there will be overtones and associations that are slightly different. Three common words which seem completely interchangeable are 'begin', 'start' and 'commence'. Yet a sensitive writer will be aware that there is a sharpness and vigour about 'start' which the other two are lacking, while 'commence' has a certain dignity not to be found in the other two. The long words in the list above have their place and uses. They only become an obstacle to clear English when too many are used together in a passage or when the writer chooses them in the mistaken belief that they make his work more impressive. Sometimes they are used because the writer wishes to *reduce* the impact of his words: 'he uttered a terminological inexactitude' or 'he was economical with the truth' shows the writer shying away from the plain statement, '*he told a lie*'. The short words are clear and vigorous and there is no dodging their impact. Therefore choose a short word rather than its longer equivalent unless you judge the long word more effective for a particular purpose – or have a special reason for obscuring your meaning!

3. Prefer the concrete word to the abstract

This is an extension of point 2 above. Writers in the world of business and government departments often seem happier using abstract nouns rather than their concrete equivalents: 'road transport' for 'cars and lorries'; 'financial inducements' for 'bribes'; 'industrial action' for 'strikes'; 'senior management' for 'top managers'; 'concessionary rates' for 'cheap tickets'.

The shock of using such plain English might be too much for some writers and very disturbing for some readers, but compare the impact of 'senior management has offered financial inducements to some of the union leadership to oppose industrial action' with the much more startling '*top managers have tried to bribe some union leaders to vote against a strike*'.

4. Use an active verb rather than a passive

To understand this piece of advice we have to take a short excursion into grammar. A verb is said to be 'active' when it shows someone or something actually doing something: the footballer *kicked* the ball; the cook *baked* the cake; the evidence *proved* the thief guilty; the old folk *have seen* better days. In each example the verbs are said to be 'active' and you can see how they are each conveying that someone or something is doing the action in the verb. If we now turn these verbs into the 'passive', the sentences become: the ball *was kicked* by the footballer; a cake *is baked* by the cook; the thief *was proved* guilty by the evidence; better days *have been seen* by the old folk.

In almost every case, the sentence with the active verb is the more effective. There is just one example where you might feel that the sentence with the passive verb actually has more impact. This is: 'the thief was proved guilty by the evidence'. If you prefer this version to 'the evidence proved the thief guilty', the reason for your choice lies in the next piece of advice.

5. Where possible, make a person the subject of your sentence

Of course it is not always possible to do this, but very often you can increase the effect and directness of your sentence by replacing an abstract word (such as 'evidence') with a personal word (such as 'thief'), for instance:

> 'Employment prospects in the North East are improving' could become: 'Many more people in the North East are finding employment.'

'The prevalence of whooping cough in young children is causing concern to doctors' could be better expressed as: 'Doctors are concerned about the prevalence of whooping cough in young children.' Better still would be: 'Too many young children are contracting whooping cough and doctors are concerned.'

3 Starting to Write

If you want to improve your writing you must practise it as often as you can. Don't wait until you have mastered the sections on grammar, punctuation and spelling in this book. Learn these as you go along, applying them, when necessary, to your own writing. The important thing is to get into the habit of writing so that words begin to flow easily. Accept that you will make mistakes and that at first (and perhaps for a long time) the sentences may not say exactly what you want them to. This is why you will be practising drafting and redrafting as you struggle to make the passages you write just that much clearer. By setting out to practise regularly you will only be doing what many professional writers do when they are 'between books' awaiting ideas that will lead to the next one. Many have said how they make a point of sitting at their desks for a fixed period every day and writing so many thousand words just to keep themselves in training for the next big work. What they write may well end up in the waste-paper basket, but it will have served its purpose of keeping the authors fit and ready for their next assignments.

You may have quite enough opportunities in your career or as a student to practise your writing. If you haven't, and are wondering what you could write for practice, then think about keeping a journal of your own activities. You will find advice on how to go about this in chapter 5.

Drafting and redrafting

The processes by which we write are very individual and there is no single correct method. If the end-product is excellent, it does not matter how it has been achieved. For most successful writers, however, the preliminary stages take up more time than the final draft.

If we take a practical example, we can illustrate one way of going about a writing task and show the value of drafting and redrafting.

Let's assume that you are the secretary of a twinning organization with the job of arranging visits between your town and its twin in France. The letter you are about to write will be read by your opposite number in France, who is fluent in English and will appreciate a clear statement of the problems which you foresee. The situation is that you and your committee in the UK welcome the idea of a visit by your French friends, but the dates they propose are not suitable nor are some of the activities which they have in mind. Your task is to write a very careful letter, avoiding any suggestion that the visitors will be unwelcome but conveying the difficulties and making alternative proposals.

The first stage is to write down the main points you need to make in your letter. The list may look like this:

> 12–16 October inconvenient; 19–23 preferred; coincide with Town Carnival; band welcome but programme unsuitable for church (the only venue); startled at suggestion that football team and supporters should also come; local teams of poor quality; no time to arrange better fixtures; glad the mayor is coming; will need VIP treatment; special programme fixed for him.

You now have on paper the bare facts as they occurred to you. Next you have to decide the order in which to put them to achieve the best effect. You decide that the one thing that really pleases you so far is that their mayor is coming with the party. Reference to this would make a gracious opening to the letter. You will have to deal with the change of dates early in the letter as this is vital to the arrangements, but you can make this attractive (you hope) by linking the visit with the Town Carnival. This opening should have created a sufficiently genial mood in your letter for you to embark on the delicate matters of the band's unsuitable programme and the surprise of having to cope with their crack football team.

You have already put a good deal of thought and planning into your letter. You know what you want to say and the order in which you are going to say it. You are ready to write the first draft of your letter. As you write, you will find your thoughts about the problems become clearer and new ideas put themselves forward. Your first draft might read as follows:

Dear Mme Lebrun

Thank you for your letter of 13 March concerning the visit to Twinton *of your mayor as well as your Town Band.* We look forward to welcoming them and *be assured that* there will be special visits arranged for him to local industries and the mayors of other nearby towns.

Unfortunately, however, we would be happier if your party could visit us from 19–23 October instead of the 12–16. These later dates would coincide with our Town Carnival, which is quite a spectacular show. *Your Town Band would no doubt be able to take part in these festivities.* With *regard to* their proposed programme for the concert in St Michael's church, we wonder if they have in their repertoire some more 'serious' type of music. The vicar is rather *wary of concerts* in his church and it would be tactful if the programme was not too lightweight.

The suggestion of a football team coming is a great surprise and *the players will be made most welcome. We would draw your attention to the fact that* there are no teams in this area of the standard of your famous team. *Perhaps we could suggest that a special football tour could be arranged in the South of England for next spring.* This, we are sure, would be more suitable and satisfactory to all concerned. *However, if they want to visit Twinton just for a holiday of course they can come along.*

We shall look forward to hearing your comments on these various proposals.
Yours sincerely

. . . .

This is not a bad start but there are eleven places where the wording could be improved. These are printed in italic in the above letter.

1 It is a mistake to deal with both the mayor and the Town Band in the opening paragraph, especially as the band's programme is causing problems. Use the first paragraph to welcome the mayor and leave the band until later.

2 The phrase *be assured that* is rather pompous and could be expressed more simply.

3 The two adverbs, *Unfortunately, however,* make a very clumsy opening to the second paragraph.

4 As you wrote the draft, it occurred to you that the band could take part in the Carnival procession. You should make the invitation to do so more specific.

5 *With regard to* is one of those pompous phrases which should be replaced by something more simple.

6 *Wary of concerts* is vague, especially to a foreign reader. Be more explicit.

7 To say *the players will be made most welcome* is insincere, since you are going to suggest that they postpone their visit. You will need to rephrase this tactfully in order to avoid giving offence.

8 *We would draw your attention to the fact that* is wordy and sounds like an old-fashioned letter from the Inland Revenue!

9 Your new suggestion of a special football tour next spring needs more explanation.

10 *. . . they can come along.* The sentence which ends in this way is too casual when compared with the semi-formal style of the rest of the letter.

11 *We shall look forward to hearing your comments on these various proposals* is not necessarily wrong, but it lacks any personal warmth. It would be better to leave your French reader with a more friendly and encouraging message.

In our second draft of this letter, we will try to adopt a more friendly and personal tone, avoiding any hint of business jargon and improving on the points noted above:

Dear Mme Lebrun

I was very pleased to receive your letter of the 13 March and to learn that all is going well for your visit to Twinton. It is particularly good news that the Mayor of Touville is coming with the party. Our local committee is already preparing a special programme for him. He will be officially welcomed by our own mayor and there will be courtesy visits to the mayors of two neighbouring towns. He will also be shown our new industrial estate.

There is one important point I must discuss with you. It concerns the dates of your visit. You have proposed 12–16 October. This is quite possible for us, but if you came a few days later – 19–23 October – you would coincide with our Carnival Week. This is always a great local event and we would like our French guests to share it with us. I am sure you and your party would enjoy the various activities. We would be especially pleased if your excellent Town Band could march in the carnival procession.

We are much looking forward to the band concert in our church of St Michael. I have read the proposed programme, which looks delightful. There is, however, one request. Could you suggest to the conductor that the selection of pop tunes at the end of the evening might be unsuitable for a concert in a church? The vicar welcomes concerts in St Michael's but always insists on classical music. I am sure you understand.

Your proposal to bring your football team with you is a great surprise. The players themselves would of course be very welcome, but I am afraid that our local teams are not up to the standard of your team and would be unable to provide any worthwhile opposition. If we were given more time, I know my committee would be very happy to arrange a special tour for your team – say, next spring – visiting some larger towns in this region to play against teams more experienced than ours. Perhaps you would like to discuss this with the football club officials and let me know their reaction.

I am glad the arrangements for this exchange visit are developing well. The committee and the host families are greatly looking forward to seeing our French friends again. I shall be glad to know what you think about the dates we propose and also the possibility of a football tour in the Spring.

Yours sincerely

. . . .

This letter is a distinct improvement on the first one. The tone is more friendly, the points clearer and we have avoided pompous jargon. It could be sent to France with some confidence.

Summary

Get into the habit of writing. Regular practice is essential for ease of expression and writing a journal is an excellent way to practise your writing.

It is essential to spend time on the planning stage.

Think about what you want to say and jot down the main points. Arrange these in the most effective order.

Consider who is to read what you write and decide the style best suited for your reader(s) and your material.

Write a first draft, bearing in mind that the very act of writing will force you to clarify what is in your mind. Revise this draft carefully, removing clumsy phrases and ensuring that the message is as clear as you can make it.

Write a second draft. This may prove to be the final version. If it is still not satisfactory, revise it and then produce your final version. In other words, be prepared to draft and redraft until you are satisfied that you can make no further improvement.

4 Personal Style

The word 'style' is a little frightening and perhaps suggests something rather special put on for the occasion. This is not so. Style is the reflection of the personality of the writer.

When you write, let the reader hear your voice, identified by vocabulary and turns of phrase which are undoubtedly 'you'. If you try to make yourself sound impressive by using words that do not come naturally to you, the result will be the very opposite of what you hoped. The reader will quickly detect the falseness of the style and suspect a small person hiding behind the inflated language.

Your style – while remaining 'you' – will be modified according to the person for whom you are writing and the subject matter of your text, though the essential requirement of sincerity will not change. A business letter to an unknown correspondent will have a formality and impersonal tone because you are writing on behalf of an organization and are only one of many employees who will write as members of that firm. It would be unusual and certainly disturbing if the letters sent out by a firm were all in different styles reflecting the individual personalities of the many writers who work for it!

A personal letter is another matter. Here your own voice will be heard much more clearly, especially if the letter is informal and written to someone with whom you are on easy terms. Interestingly, the personal voice in a letter is not always quite the same as the voice which speaks to you face to face. Often the act of writing induces a certain carefulness in phrasing which you do not normally associate with the writer. Sometimes, however, the reverse is true and we are surprised at the casualness and scrappy writing of a friend who has always struck us as rather correct in manner of speech.

The act of writing has revealed another side to the character. This should lead us to consider the impression we are conveying when we write: does our style – that is, our manner of writing – assist or detract from the effectiveness of our message? Is it appropriate for the task in hand? Will the reader subconsciously accept it or will it put him off? These questions apply to all writing and should be in your mind whatever you are drafting, whether it is a letter (business or personal), a report, a set of minutes, a college essay — or a five-hundred page novel!

5 Writing a Journal

There is no restriction on what one can put into a journal and this is what makes it such an attractive framework for someone who wants to practise all kinds of writing but cannot think how to begin. Essentially a journal is a record of what you do and what you think from day to day, although there is no need to make an entry every day if you do not want to. You can decide to write something in your journal every two or three days or once a week, but it would be as well to impose upon yourself the discipline of regular writing. If you wait for inspiration, you may never write anything at all!

Look back over your day or week and find something in it that interested you and then write about this while it is fresh in your mind. The length of the entry will be your decision, sometimes just a few lines and at other times as much as two or three pages. Very probably the short entry will be the one that causes you the most trouble, either because you have less material or because you are trying to say something important to you in a very few words. Your entry may be a factual account of something you did; it may be the thoughts and emotions evoked by a certain place you have visited or of a character you have met; it may be your thoughts on a topic that has caught your attention, or it may be your hopes and plans for the future. You can see that there is no need to be at a loss for something to write in your journal!

Although the words 'journal' and 'diary' are often regarded as interchangeable, there is a distinction. A diary is much more a list of events, even though a famous diarist such as Samuel Pepys comments at length when he feels inclined. A journal, on the other hand, implies a less rigid approach than a diary, with more room for reflection and variety of subject matter. As your aim is to practise your writing, avoid the temptation to fill your journal with jottings and abbreviations that often suffice for diary entries.

A journal is such a personal thing that it may be surprising to suggest that you should envisage a reader. Yet this is always a basic requirement when you begin writing. It is quite possible to choose yourself as the reader and, like many writers of journals, write for no other person than yourself, who several years hence may enjoy reliving experiences which would otherwise have been totally forgotten. An alternative would be to think that you are writing your journal for a friend who is a long way away and to whom you want to give an insight into your life. You might imagine instead that your journal will be read by your grandchildren a long way into the future and you want to convey to them a flavour of life today as you are experiencing it. Your choice of a potential reader will subtly alter the way you write. If you are writing only for yourself, you will be able to omit a great deal of detail that would be necessary if you are writing for someone who is at a distance from you in place or time. In writing for your grandchildren you will have to remember that things will be very different in their day and many things you take for granted will need full explanation for their benefit.

It is by no means easy to capture the fleeting moment or passing emotion in words. You may be writing about a family reunion. The actual events will not prove too difficult to record, but when you wish to express the feelings that came and went during them, you may find yourself facing a considerable challenge to find just the right words to say what you mean. You can provide yourself with a framework by noting in rough the main sequence of events and making sure they are in the right order. You might also jot down against each one the emotions you felt, but it will be in the *writing of* your *first draft* that you will have to clarify your remembered feelings – pleasure, anxiety, excitement, jealousy, or whatever they may be. This is an example of *thinking while writing* that we have spoken of before. It may need several attempts before you honestly say you have come near expressing exactly what you felt.

As your journal is intended to give you as much practice as possible in writing, vary the topics you write about. One day may afford you the opportunity for a piece of descriptive writing, another for a factual account of events, another for some reminiscing and another for recording something practical, such as a new recipe that proved particularly successful. If you are serious about your journal, you may look back in some months or years ahead and find that what set out to be an excuse for practising written English has turned into a valued document about a certain period of your life.

Here are two examples of entries in a personal journal. The first gives the writer the opportunity to attempt a character sketch within a narrative framework and the second gives scope for descriptive writing.

Friday 25 March

Today I am recovering from our visit to Harlow. 'Come and meet my new flat-mate,' said my daughter brightly. As an afterthought, she added, 'You'll love her.'

Did I detect a slight air of doubt in that assertion? Daughter Jane well knows my opinion of her previous flat-mates: Miranda the sulky and Vanessa the slut (I use the term only to describe one who never washed the dishes, the bathroom basin or the kitchen floor – and herself only rarely). Perhaps Kathy would be different.

She was! An absolutely splendid girl, cheerful, friendly and thoroughly likeable. It was her father who was the trouble. I never expected him to be there when I arrived. Apparently he had brought an old black and white TV set which he thought that Kathy might like to have. It was obvious that she did not want that television in her flat – nor her father! You could understand why. The man was a bore.

He insisted on setting up the TV there and then (despite the fact that there was a better one already installed). First he had to search the flat for a plug and then find tools to fix it on to the lead. Next he erected a totally unnecessary aerial and finally moved several pieces of furniture in order to place that wretched TV where he thought it should go. As if all this were not bad enough, he kept up a running commentary about his own skills as a handyman and how lucky our Jane was to have a flat-mate with a father who was so willing to undertake all the little jobs 'that girls can't do'. I was proud of Jane. She behaved with great restraint and even managed a word of insincere thanks through gritted teeth. But it was Kathy whom I admired even more.

As I was present, she had to tolerate her father fixing up that television, but once he had done so she made it absolutely clear – even to him – that it was time for him to go. She followed him out to his car and, from the window, we saw her having a few words with him. Then she came back into the house, disappeared into the kitchen and returned a few minutes later with a tray laden with tea and cakes. She was smiling.

'Sorry about that,' she said genially. 'Don't worry. He won't be around here again in a hurry.'

We were both dying to know what she had said to him and Jane horrified me by asking her.

'Have some more cake,' Kathy replied.

We took the hint and nothing more was said about it.
But I would love to know what she told him.

Monday 4 April

After work I went to fetch the dog back from the kennels. We had been away for a few days and had decided it was best not to take him with us. Car journeys and unfamiliar hotels do not appeal to him.

I always enjoy going out to the kennels. They are seven miles out into the country and I love the drive, especially at this time of year. Last Monday was one of those days of early April when summer seems to have arrived three months early. The sky was a powdery blue, the late afternoon sun positively sultry and only the daffodils and the hardly unfurled leaves on the hedges and trees reminded you that it was still quite early spring.

There was no traffic at all on the country road and I could imagine I was back in the 1920s, when motoring was a pleasure, purring along in an open car with time to look at the scenery or draw into a gateway and stare at the landscape. Why not do that now? I said to myself – and pulled into the next convenient opening.

I did not regret it. Patterned with greens and browns and a touch of Devon red, the fields fell away below me to a large wood that ran right across the valley floor. It stretched for a good half mile before gradually ascending the further slope. Beyond it rose the tors of Dartmoor, hazy now as a light mist brought the first hint of evening to the furthest hills. I allowed myself a full five minutes to enjoy the scene, puffing my pipe like a character in a J. B. Priestley novel. Then I remembered our dog and suddenly felt guilty that he was behind bars while I was relishing the freedom of the countryside. I got into the car and drove off – yes, I have to say it – into the sunset.

Summary

Keeping a journal is excellent practice in the art of writing. The length of each entry is your decision, but avoid turning your journal into a series of jottings.

Envisage a reader – even if it is only yourself in twenty years' time!

Use your journal to practise various kinds of writing: factual accounts, descriptions, reminiscences, imaginative pieces, etc.

6 Writing Letters

The commonest form of writing any of us indulge in is the writing of letters. The Post Office handles millions of letters every year and, despite the telephone, the numbers are always on the increase. This is a form of writing where clear English is at a premium. When you have written your letter, what you have said you have said – for better or for worse! In business, a badly written letter may mean a lost order or a lost customer; in a personal letter, a lost friend or a family crisis. It is too late to say, when the letter has been sent, 'I didn't mean that.'

The impression your letter makes begins the moment it is unfolded from its envelope – sooner perhaps, because the appearance of the envelope and the way it is addressed is already saying something about the sender. Before a word of your letter is read, the layout of the sheet, the quality of the handwriting or typing – even the texture of the paper – are sending messages to the reader. These messages are twofold: they say something about you and (even more important) they are revealing what you think of the person to whom you are writing!

A casually written or badly typed letter shows that you do not care very much about what the reader thinks of you; it also shows that you do not think he or she is worth much effort on your part. This is insulting and the sender of such a letter should not be surprised if offence is taken. Perhaps the worst form of this is when you write to someone asking for information and the person replies by sending you back your *own letter* with a reply scribbled along the bottom. Never allow yourself to do this. It shows a great lack of courtesy.

Courtesy is a keyword in the writing of letters and it is especially important in the writing of business correspondence. It is implicit in every good business letter that you assume the person you are addressing to be someone of importance and someone to be treated with politeness and consideration. The high-handed tone of some official letters understandably upsets people and in recent years the Civil Service has made great efforts to write to people in a way that is much more human than the condescending style of former times.

(It is ironic that the pompous phrases of olden days such as 'I remain your obedient servant' really meant 'I consider myself highly superior to you!')

Although the body of the letter is 'the cream of the correspondence' (a delightful phrase used by Tony Lumpkin in Goldsmith's *She Stoops to Conquer*), the layout of the letter is important. As already mentioned, people in the business world will judge a firm by its letters and they expect certain conventions to be observed. The way a letter is set out *is* conventional – that is to say, it follows a pattern generally accepted to be correct, even though there may be several other ways of doing it. The advantage of following convention is that you know what is expected of you and how to do it. Once a convention has been established it is taken for granted that any other way is wrong and anyone who deviates is ignorant of how to do the job properly. No one wants to be thought ignorant and so we all conform!

Having said that, it is worth remarking that conventions do change. For example, many years ago a great deal of punctuation was expected around the headings of letters (the addresses, etc.) and at the signing. Nowadays it is common practice to leave out all punctuation in these places, especially when the letter is typed. Again, the date has usually appeared under your address at the top right of the page. Now in some business letters it is appearing on the *left* side. It is therefore as well to keep an eye on the layout of letters you receive from large organizations. From time to time you may detect a slight change in the conventions which you would be wise to adopt.

The conventions

Personal letters

The layout of a personal letter must be well-known to you already. You write your address in the top right-hand corner of the notepaper with the date below it. It is customary to indent each successive line of the address to give a 'tapered' appearance, as in the example below. You begin the letter 'Dear . . . ,' (note the comma after the name) and you end the letter 'Yours sincerely,' (also followed by a comma, as you see). You may conclude with a less formal greeting such as 'Love,' 'Yours ever,' or whatever is appropriate for that particular letter to that correspondent.

The informality of family letters or those between close friends is such that you can decide for yourself how much you bother with conventions. But personal letters may be written to acquaintances where a certain degree of formality is required. In these cases, you should make sure that you sign off using the correct style – which is 'Yours sincerely'. Remember to use a capital Y for 'Yours' and a small s for 'sincerely' followed by a comma. Then your legible signature should be written below. Here is an example of a letter written to someone you know personally but not as an intimate friend nor as a member of your family:

> 42, Valley Drive,
> Stokely,
> Wiltshire,
> XY3 2AB.
> 24 June 1989

Dear Mrs Boston,

Thank you very much for allowing us to visit your beautiful gardens last weekend. My family and our American guest spent a highly enjoyable afternoon at 'The Cedars' and we are particularly indebted to your gardener, Mr Anstey, who gave us a most interesting conducted tour. We were sorry not to meet you again, but Mr Anstey explained that you had to go to London at short notice. We hope very much to see you when you return. Perhaps this will be at next month's meeting of the Gardening Club.

> Yours sincerely,
> Joan Ponting

You will notice that each line of your address in the top right-hand corner ends with a comma, except the last one which has a full stop. This is a long-established convention and is still quite correct. However, neither the commas nor the full stop add anything to the clarity of the address and nowadays they are no longer regarded as essential and you will find many correspondents who omit them; but if you are using a comma after 'Dear . . .' and after 'Yours sincerely' it would look better to continue to use the commas and full stop in your address on the grounds of consistency if nothing else. You also have to consider the person to whom you are writing. If you feel that he or she would expect to see full punctuation, then you should include it. On the other hand, your reader might be the sort of person to favour a more streamlined approach and for him or her you could leave out all the punctuation in these places, as in a modern business letter. You may think that this style looks better when the letter is typed and that a hand-written letter should follow the older style of full punctuation. This really is a 'grey' area at present where your own judgement has to operate. It might be safest to say that when you write by hand you include all the punctuation in the heading and the ending, but that when you use a typewriter for a personal letter you can choose to use all the punctuation or none. The important thing is to be consistent within the letter: if you punctuate some lines but fail to do so elsewhere, it looks as if you do not know what you are doing!

Business letters

The layout of a business letter differs from that of a personal letter in two important ways: (a) you include the *name* and the *address* of your correspondent on the left of the page above 'Dear . . .' and (b) you sign off as 'Yours faithfully'. Here is a short example which we can discuss:

Tel. 0321-1234

Holton House
Holton Road
Leston
Devon
AB3 4JK
25 April 1989

The Manager
Techno Industries Plc
The Trading Estate
Uptown
Lomeshire
BX4 3AL

Dear Sir

Thank you for your letter of 20 April 1989 inviting me to visit you on 1 May to discuss the development of my new invention. I will look forward to meeting you at your office at 11.30 a.m. as you suggested.

Yours faithfully

This is the kind of business letter that you as an individual might write to a firm. Your home address is in the top right corner. It is not customary to put your name above your address, although you sometimes see it — especially if the writer sticks on a personal address label instead of writing or typing the address. It is best to avoid using the stick-on label for important letters. You must, however, be sure to write the name or title (in this example, 'The Manager') of your correspondent above his or her address. This part of the heading is never indented as your own address may be, but each line begins exactly under the one above it.

You will notice that no punctuation is used in the headings and the signing-off and that each paragraph is not indented but begins at the left-hand margin, as does 'Yours faithfully'. Punctuation is used in the body of the letter of course, but modern practice is to be as sparing of it as possible so that the page is not spattered with unnecessary commas. Be sure, though, that all the full stops are in place. These are the most essential pieces of punctuation and their absence or incorrect use will suggest ignorance on the part of the writer.

One example of changing conventions is the way that the date seems to be moving away from its traditional place under your address to a position above or below the name and address of your correspondent. The placing of your telephone number offers some choice too. Many people now place it under their address. A heading illustrating these two changes is as follows:

> Holton House
> Holton Road
> Leston
> Devon
> AB3 4JK
> Tel. 0321-1234

25 April 1989

The Manager
Techno Industries Plc
The Trading Estate
Uptown
Lomeshire
BX4 3AL

Dear Sir

You may wish to write a letter to a firm without specifying the person (e.g. the manager or the secretary) who is to read it. In this case, begin 'Dear Sirs'. There is a problem if you do not know if your reader will be a man or woman. The customary way out of this dilemma is to write 'Dear Sir/Madam'.

Very often you will be writing a business letter to a person whose name you know. This may well come about when you are replying to a business letter. You opened the correspondence with a formal 'Dear Sir' and you received a reply which addressed you by name ('Dear Mr Marston'). The writer signed the letter with his name and quite correctly used 'Yours sincerely' since he had made his letter person-to-person. When you write back to him, you would still write the heading in business letter style, but instead of addressing it to 'The Manager', you would use his name both in the heading and after 'Dear . . .' To continue to address him as 'Dear Sir' would be an error and an impoliteness. You should end your letter 'Yours sincerely'.

There is a helpful piece of advice if uncertainty about how to reply still lingers, and that is to copy the manner in which you have been addressed. If for any reason the firm retains the impersonal style in its reply to you and therefore addresses you as 'Sir' or 'Madam', ending 'Yours faithfully', you would do well to retain this style when you write to them again. But most probably you will find your name being used and this is the signal for you to continue the exchange of letters addressing your correspondent by name.

So far we have considered you as an individual who is writing a business letter to a firm. On the other hand, you may be the person in the office writing the letters on behalf of the firm. The general principles of writing such business letters are the same as those outlined above. One big difference, however, is that your firm will almost certainly have headed notepaper and the placing of your telephone (and telex) number will have been decided for you. In your initial training you should also be told such details as where the office expects the date to be written and the references – both yours and your correspondent's – to be placed. Sometimes the subject of the letter is written as a kind of heading on the line below 'Dear . . .' This is an example of a letter that might be sent out from a large firm:

THE TRANSCON TRANSPORT CO. LTD
WHELTON
LOMESHIRE
LO2 PN3

Tel. 0473-8976

Our reference JMB/IG
Your reference NHG/HJ

27 March 1989

The Manager
Sweetlands Confections Ltd
Old Street
Newtown
Sussex
NE5 OT4

Dear Sir

<u>Contract Renewal</u>

I enclose a list of the revised charges for our transport of perishable goods as from 1 January of next year. We regret the small rise in costs but have managed to limit it to the annual rate of inflation. Our representative will be happy to discuss this and any other queries you may have when he calls on you, as arranged, on the 28th of this month.

Yours faithfully

P. Stirling
Contracts Manager

Enclosure

The final word 'Enclosure' is added to show that another document has been sent in addition to the letter. It also reminds the sender's secretary to enclose it!

If your typed letter is a long one and two or more pages are required, then the last word on the text of a page is repeated after an oblique stroke at the bottom right-hand corner. At the top of the next page the stroke and the word are typed once more. An alternative is to type the word 'continued . . .' at the bottom of the first page and repeat it at the top of the next. In these ways the reader is directed to the following pages and has no difficulty in linking together parts of an interrupted sentence or paragraph.

Addressing the envelope

An easy enough job, surely? True, since very little mental effort is required to write someone's name and address on an envelope. We should bear in mind, however, that the envelope containing the letter is part of the communication in that it is conveying to the recipient an impression of the sender. A carelessly addressed envelope is a poor introduction to the letter within.

The address should be typed or written clearly in the middle of the envelope, leaving enough space for the large commemorative stamps that are sold by the Post Office these days. Each line of the address can be blocked directly under the one above it, or each line can be indented. A comma at the end of each line and a full stop after the final word are still to be seen on envelopes but, following the modern custom of doing away with unnecessary clutter in letters and on envelopes, punctuation is very commonly omitted.

There has been a move away from addressing every male as Esq. (short for 'Esquire'), a courteous suggestion that every man receiving a letter is a member of the minor gentry. It is still frequently used and is quite correct and even desirable if you want to include a touch of harmless flattery on the envelope. But the plainer and more honest 'Mr' is quite acceptable and commonly used. To address a woman (on the envelope or in the letter) whose marital status is unknown to you, the title 'Ms' has come into use.

The Post Office issues guidelines on the addressing of envelopes to help them sort and deliver our letters efficiently. It regards the post town as the most important word on the envelope and that is why the word is often underlined and/or written in capital letters to draw attention to it. The county is also required since there may be more than one town of that name in the country. Automatic sorting makes the use of the post-code essential. To omit it might mean a delay for your letter. A correctly addressed envelope might look like this:

> Mr J. Higgins
> 25 Lower Dock Street
> West Hoe
> PLYMSTON
> Devon
> PL1 DP3

Style in business letters

There was a time when people in offices felt they had to make their organizations (and themselves) appear impressive by using high-flown language, complicated sentences and a special vocabulary of business terms. Instead of saying the 13th of this month or simply giving that date, they wrote *the 13th instant*. For the 13th of last month they wrote *the 13th ultimo* – and next month was *proxime*! The abbreviations for these terms may still be seen in use occasionally: *inst, ult, prox*. Goods were never sent; they were *dispatched*. The office never received letters: it was *in receipt of* them. You may still come across examples of this useless pomposity, but the tendency now is towards directness and simplicity. These are highly desirable qualities but not necessarily easy to achieve. To begin with, your attitude of mind towards your correspondent should be helpful and friendly and you should not treat him or her as someone to be talked down to. Suppose you had rung up your local library and asked for a certain book on Egyptian history. Compare your reactions to these two versions of the librarian's reply:

Dear Sir

With reference to your telephone communication of the 12th ultimo, which has just been brought to my notice, I have to inform you that the volume you have requested ('Egyptian History' – B. Falda) is no longer located at this branch, but has to be obtained for you on written application through the inter-library loan service. If you would favour us with such a written request, we will put the matter in hand forthwith. I feel it incumbent on me, however, to warn you that, owing to a large number of requests for the volume you are seeking, delivery may be delayed for several weeks. I will make my best endeavours to expedite this matter when I am in receipt of your instructions.
Assuring you of our best attention,
I beg to remain,
Yours faithfully,

P. Butcher
Librarian

Dear Mr Jones
Thank you for your phone message of 12 June, which has just been passed to me. I am afraid that we no longer have a copy of 'Egyptian History' by B. Falda at this branch. We can, however, order it for you through the inter-loan service if you send us a request in writing. The book is very much in demand and we may have to wait several weeks for it. We will of course do all we can to get the book for you as soon as possible.
Yours sincerely

L. Baker
Librarian.

After reading the first letter, you probably feel that the library is remote and condescending, despite the protestation of giving you the 'best attention'. The long words and official jargon obscure rather than clarify the message and the whole intention seems to be to make you feel how important the librarian is and how inferior you are.

The second letter is very different. The librarian addresses you by name and adopts a friendly personal tone. He avoids jargon and adopts a simple vocabulary. The letter is businesslike but the tone is encouraging and you feel that the librarian is taking an interest in you and will do all he can to help you obtain the book you want. His response is clear, courteous, businesslike yet friendly! How do you cultivate these qualities in your business letters?

As in all kinds of writing, you must begin by being clear in your own mind what you want to say. Even if the letter is quite short and merely passing on or seeking a single piece of information, you should jot this down on your notepad and look at it. Have you really got down all that is necessary? Is there no additional point you should add to make it clearer? Put yourself in the position of your correspondent and ask yourself if your letter provides all the information needed.

With a complicated letter there is all the more reason for planning out your points before you compose the letter. Noting down the points will allow you to put them in the best order and supply back-up details to clarify your message. Remember that items such as dates, times, catalogue numbers, references to previous letters and suchlike are vital to the effect of the letter. A remark such as 'I want to inquire about those goods you sold me a week or two ago and which I wrote to you about' would not elicit a very prompt response, whereas a letter specifying the goods, the catalogue numbers, the date of purchase and the date of your previous letter would enable action to be taken immediately. Put yourself in the place of your reader and think what he or she needs to be told. This attitude will also help you to develop the necessary courteous tone. However upset you may be over some piece of inefficiency or bad administration, you are likely to achieve more by remaining calm and polite. There are occasions when someone deserves a really strong letter, but even this should not overstep the bounds. From a practical point of view, you are likely to gain more if you maintain your dignity and do not lose your temper at the typewriter! The temptation to write an angry letter is probably quite rare. Most business letters are routine affairs written to enable something to be done. Assume that your correspondent is a reasonable, sensible person, worthy of respect and consideration, and phrase your letter accordingly.

The businesslike style will be achieved if you keep your mind on the essentials of what you want to stay and stick to them. The essentials may be so brief that your letter looks too short to send. This will not be so. Providing you begin and end in a suitably gracious way, there is absolutely no need to pad out the letter just because it seems to be rather short. A clear message, well set out and politely phrased, is all that can be desired from you.

How to begin a letter

'Once I get started I'm all right, but I never know how to begin.' This is a very common feeling. Perhaps you have memories of writing essays at school and being told to write a good introduction. This may or may not be good advice for a school essay, but it is completely unnecessary for a business letter. The best advice is to take your first point and launch into it straight away. This is often acknowledging the receipt of the letter to which you are replying, and so you would begin 'Thank you for your letter of 3 September 1989 ordering twenty cases of . . . etc.' You would have quoted the reference of their letter in the heading (as shown above) and from this and from your opening sentence the reader would have no difficulty in finding the correspondence and knowing exactly why you are writing.

If your letter is opening the correspondence, then stating what you want or why you are writing in the first sentence or two is the most efficient way of going about things. It depends of course on your purpose in writing – ordering goods, making an inquiry, registering a complaint, applying for a job, requesting payment, arranging an appointment and so on. Here is an opening sentence for each of these possibilities. You will notice that each sentence comes to the point straight away:

Dear Sir/Madam

(a) Will you please send me a flash attachment for my camera (make . . .; catalogue number . . .)?

(b) Would you be kind enough to send me details of the holiday weekend for campers in Brittany, as advertised yesterday in the local press?

(c) I purchased a model 303 vacuum cleaner from you last Saturday, 23 February, but it broke down within two days.

(d) I wish to apply for the post of housekeeper at Mardon Lodge, as advertised last night in the 'Somerset Star'.

(e) I am rendering my account for the repairs to your house, which were completed three months ago.

You will have noticed the polite approach in (a) and (b). A phrase such as 'would you be kind enough' or 'would you be good enough' is a courteous way of asking someone to do something for you. The writers of (c) and (e) have less reason to feel gracious: one has been sold faulty goods and the other has not been paid for three months after finishing a job. All the same, they restrain their displeasure and content themselves with a plain statement of their complaint, which speaks for itself.

Another useful phrase to launch you into your topic is 'I am writing . . .' For example, (c) might have begun, 'I am writing to complain about a model 303 vacuum cleaner which I bought . . . etc.' From opening sentences such as this and the ones shown above it should be easy to continue the letter, adding whatever further points are necessary. Then it should be concluded with some suitable remark before being signed and sent.

How to end a letter

What is a 'suitable remark' for the ending of a letter? This depends on the response you hope to gain from your correspondent, but you will not achieve the best result if you leave the reader with a feeling that you have been abrupt or uncivil. Therefore, a suitable closing remark is essential. If you are hoping for a reply, a common ending is 'I look forward to hearing from you.' This suggests that you will be pleased to continue the correspondence – although there might be a hint of menace within it if you have asked for an explanation of something that has made you cross! Perhaps your letter has asked for information or advice. You could end with 'I would be grateful for any help you can give me.' A job application often ends with 'If you wish to interview me, I can be available at any time convenient to you.' Alternatively, you might conclude with a sentence such as, 'I trust my application will be of interest to you.' A letter to a customer often ends with 'Assuring you of our best attention'. (One hopes that the writer means it!) It is quite possible that the content of your letter will lead straight on to 'Yours faithfully' or 'Yours sincerely' without the necessity for one of these closing remarks, but it is important to check that such an ending reads smoothly and agreeably. If it seems sudden and unfriendly, then find a concluding sentence that will round off your letter pleasantly and encourage the response you desire.

Examples of business letters

These two letters are given as examples of an exchange of business correspondence, correctly set out and written in clear English. It should be stressed that there are perfectly acceptable variations of these layouts and more than one way of phrasing the messages! However, these letters follow widely accepted conventions and would be considered efficient communications in the business world of today.

Let's assume that you are organizing a youth band and have been given a substantial grant with which to buy some instruments. You want to order two trumpets and a trombone straight away, but are uncertain which bassoons are the best buy. Your letter is to place an order for the trumpets and trombone and also to inquire about the bassoons. The firm replies acknowledging your order and giving the information about the other instruments. This is a situation where a private individual representing a small organization approaches a large firm.

25 Onder Close
Hilltown
Derbyshire
HJ7 3AN
Tel. Hilltown 3489
25 September 1989

The Manager
Musikant Instrument Supplies Ltd
Attwood Road
Oxford
OX2 8JS

Dear Sir

Thank you for your letter of 20 September giving me details of your 'hire and buy' scheme for school and youth bands and also enclosing your catalogue of instruments. I would like to order on behalf of the Hilltown Youth Band the following:

One trumpet (ref. TR305)
One trumpet (ref. TR402)
One trombone (ref. Trom218)

We would like to avail ourselves of your 'hire and buy' scheme. Would you be good enough to send the necessary documents to the Youth Band secretary at the above address?

I would also like your advice on bassoons. We are unfamiliar with the makes you have listed and would be glad to know which model you consider most suitable for a beginner.

Would you kindly let me know how soon you can deliver the instruments? I look forward to hearing from you.

Yours faithfully

John Lilton
(Conductor: Hilltown Youth Band)

MUSIKANT INSTRUMENTS SUPPLIES LTD
ATTWOOD ROAD
OXFORD
OX2 8JS

Our Ref. ABD/NK   Tel. 0865-9876
Your Ref. . . .

2 October 1989

John Lilton Esq.
25 Onder Close
Hilltown
Derbyshire
HJ7 3AN

Dear Mr Lilton

Thank you for your letter of 25 September. The two trumpets and the trombone which you ordered will be dispatched by rail within the next seven days and should reach you by 3 October at the latest. The invoice and 'hire and buy' forms will be sent at the same time to your secretary as requested. A very popular bassoon for the beginner is the BA831, but the slightly more expensive model BA847 has additional keys that would be of use to the learner who goes on to more advanced playing. From our experience this is the model we would recommend. At present we do not have a BA847 in stock but we are expecting supplies of this instrument from Germany in the next month and could despatch one to you as soon as the consignment arrives. At present we have the less expensive BA831 in stock. If you let us know which model you prefer we will do our best to send it to you as soon as possible.

We would be happy to give you any further advice you may require.

Yours sincerely

W. Rilton
(Manager)

Letters of application

You are placing evidence about yourself in the hands of a potential employer when you send a letter of application for a job. He or she will want to know a good deal about you before you are offered the job and this will be found out from your CV and from the interview (if you obtain one). But the letter of application is the first thing the employer sees and from this he or she will gain the first impression. That is why some employers ask for the letter to be in your own handwriting. An illegible scrawl may be the mark of a genius but it would not recommend itself to an employer who is looking for a conscientious assistant in the office. Handwriting, spelling, grammar and layout all make an effect on the reader and so does clear and simple phrasing in the body of the letter.

How much you write about yourself and your qualifications depends on whether or not you are enclosing a CV – a curriculum vitae. This is a summary of details about yourself, your education and your experience, set out under separate headings. CVs are frequently used these days since they enable employers to assess very rapidly the background of applicants. Well-prepared CVs make an excellent impression. A specimen is printed after the next letter, which would accompany it.

If you are sending a CV, the letter of application can be quite brief since all the important information will be contained in the CV itself. You might, however, use the letter to draw attention to anything in your background likely to be of very special interest to your employer, such as recent experience or training in the techniques required.

Glen Orion
Townsend Road
Sandford
Devon
EX4 1BJ
Tel. 0361-3489
21 May 1989

The Personnel Manager
Meadow Wine Supplies Ltd
Dock Lane
Easing
Devon EX7 2JR

Dear Sir

I wish to apply for the post of Senior Sales Assistant as advertised in the 'Devon Courier' last Thursday. I enclose my CV which I hope will interest you.

You will see that I have worked in the wine trade for seven years and have recently taken part in the sales training scheme organized by Malton Breweries. I enjoy my present work but feel I am now ready to undertake greater responsibility than my job currently offers.

I can make myself available for interview at any time you find convenient.

I look forward to hearing from you.

Yours faithfully

J. H. Jones

enclosure

Curriculum vitae

The CV is an exercise in Clear English reduced to its barest and most assimilable form. It deals in facts about you, set out in note form and usually without your further comments. A potential employer wants basic information about you and this is what the CV should provide. If it interests him, he will then go on to make personal assessment of you in an interview. What the CV contains and the way you set it out will decide whether or not you win that interview. Of course there are various ways in which the CV can be laid out but it should contain personal details about you, your education and training, previous experience and – if likely to be relevant – your outside interests. Here is what John Jones's CV might look like:

Name	John Henry Jones
Address	Glen Orion, Townsend Road, Sandford, Devon
Telephone	0361-3489
Nationality	British
Date of Birth	2 December 1963
Status	Single
EDUCATION	
1974–80	King Edward's School, Oldtown
1980–82	Plynton College of FE
	O level grade Cs in Maths, English, Art, Chemistry
	CSE 1 in General Science
	A level grade D in Economics
Courses	Sales Training – Malton Breweries 1988
EMPLOYMENT	
July 1982–Oct 1986	Olds Wine Stores, Broadway, Sandford
Oct 1986–present	Green & Guest, Vintners, High St., Exton
Position	Sales Assistant (junior)
Salary	£4025 p.a.

This is not the only way of presenting a CV. An older applicant might make more impression by following personal details with a section on Experience and Skills, while a younger person might decide that Career Aims should be set out as soon as possible. *Job*

Hunting by Alfred Hossack (Penguin, 1989) contains a lengthy section on how to plan a CV for maximum impact and gives numerous
examples illustrating different kinds of approaches.

Letters of complaint

This kind of letter has two functions: it enables you to
blow off steam about something that has dissatisfied you and it asks
for the matter to be put right. To be effective, you must keep the first
function firmly under control. Writing a rude letter may be emotion-
ally satisfying but it will not make the recipient very sympathetic to
your distress. It might even provoke a quite hostile response and
you will not achieve the main purpose of the letter, which is to
correct what has gone wrong. The important thing is to set out the
facts of the matter simply and clearly and suggest what action you
expect your correspondent to take. As in other kinds of writing, it is
a good idea to put down in rough the main points of your complaint
and then make sure they are in the best order for easy understanding
of the situation. Remember to note down relevant details, such as
the date of purchase of an article, the catalogue or model number
and a quite specific description of what has gone wrong. From these
rough notes you can compose your letter, concluding with what you
expect from the person or firm to whom you are writing.

Sometimes you may have a grievance but not be entirely sure
that your complaint will be upheld. You think you are justified in
complaining but cannot be certain of the outcome. In such a case,
you should avoid making threatening noises and firm demands. It
would be better to set out the evidence as clearly and as persuasively
as you can and then invite your correspondent to consider it and
(you hope) react in your favour. The following is an example of this
kind of letter. The writer feels hard done by, but recognizes his
ignorance of the regulations. However, he thinks it worth a try and
so writes his letter of complaint, politely suggesting that the railways
might consider making him a refund.

Moreton House
Lower Road
Moreton
Surrey MO2 3XQ
6 January 1989

The Traffic Manager
BR (South East region)
Liverpool Street Station
London

Dear Sir

I am writing to complain about being made to pay £11
excess fare on the 8.30 a.m. train from Ipswich to London
last Friday. I had bought two day-return tickets from
Ipswich to Liverpool Street at a cost (with rail cards) of
£9.40 each. I was not told of any restriction on the use of
these tickets when I purchased them; I could see no notice
forbidding us to travel on certain trains; the display
screens announcing the 8.30 a.m. train made no reference
to this and the station announcer said nothing to suggest
that day-returns were not available on this service.
In view of all this, I feel that it is unreasonable to charge
me an excess fare and would suggest that you consider
making me a refund. I enclose the receipt I was given for
the extra fare.

Yours faithfully

Summary

Conventions – Courtesy – Clarity

Conventions Use the examples given in this section to master the
conventions of layout in personal and business letters. Be alert for
changes that occur in the conventions from time to time.

Courtesy Treat your correspondents with respect and politeness, whoever they are. A well-phrased courteous letter is far more likely to achieve its aim than a carelessly written one, which will suggest that you have a low opinion of the person to whom you are sending it.

Clarity Make your message clear and easy to act on by setting it out attractively, giving all the necessary information and expressing yourself in short, well-constructed sentences.

7 Summaries

The ability to reduce a long report to a few pages of essentials is a valuable skill and one much appreciated by decision-makers. Despite the time-saving devices with which every office is equipped, no one has invented a method of speeding up the human eye and brain so that they can take in hundreds of printed words in less than hours of reading. There are techniques to enable one to read quickly but even these do not solve the time problem for a busy manager who has dozens of things to attend to and has no time to wade through pages of writing for himself. He needs an assistant who can summarize efficiently and present him with the essence of, say, a report on which he can take decisions.

For the student in higher education, summarizing is a regular necessity. To retain all the useful knowledge printed in a book is virtually impossible. The student has to identify what seems essential for his or her own purposes and find ways of keeping this available for learning and revision. The most common method is note-taking, which is a basic form of summarizing. But there are times when notes alone may not be enough and the material has to be written up in continuous prose as a coherent statement for the student's own subsequent use.

Summarizing is a technique where clear English is essential. The whole point of a summary is its clarity. It is taking the place of a long text, quite possibly closely written and dense in its material, and provides a lucid outline of the argument. It calls on the skills of clear English already discussed in this book – including short sentences and simple vocabulary wherever possible. Of course, if the matter is highly technical then one would expect technical terms to be used. We would assume that the person for whom the summary is being prepared has the necessary professional knowledge to understand what is being presented. But the purpose of your summary may be to render a technical matter accessible to a more general readership. This would mean that you would have to find non-technical equivalents for the terms employed in the original text. There is no suggestion that to be clear everything has to be reduced to basic English.

The aim is to find the essentials and reproduce them as a piece of connected writing.

Making a summary

1 The first step is to familiarize yourself with the material which you are to summarize. This sounds a far too obvious piece of advice, but it is intended to warn you against beginning to make a summary when you have read only the first sentence of the text – and students engaged in note taking sometimes make this mistake! It is much better to read a whole section of the text before you begin your summary. This will show you the line of argument the writer is taking and any special features of his style, such as highly technical vocabulary or a generous use of examples and illustrations. You will also be able to assess whether or not the text is closely packed with information (and this will make your task harder in choosing the essentials) or whether it is written in a discursive style in which really important points occur less frequently. The length of the section which you read through depends on the text. It may be the whole of a short chapter or just one section in a report. On the other hand, you may decide that four or five pages are quite enough to read initially before you go back to the beginning of your summary.

2 Take the first paragraph and read it through again so that you are familiar with what is being said. Now go through it sentence by sentence, asking yourself which sentences are saying something absolutely essential to the argument. Write down each essential point *in the form of a complete sentence*. An important reason for doing this will appear a little later on, but already it can be said that this prevents your writing down scrappy notes or single words which carry too little of the meaning.

You will recall that at the beginning of the book we made the point that the act of writing is itself a way in which we make the meaning clear to ourselves. If you challenge yourself to reproduce the point in the text in a sentence of your own wording, you are making sure that you really do understand what the writer is saying – and you cannot expect others to understand if you do not fully understand the material yourself! This would also apply if you were a student writing up the summary for your own use: you would not be writing down half digested items from the book you are studying. So be prepared to put down each essential point as a complete sentence. If you care to do so, you could number the sentences and this might be useful if you wish to retain the list simply as a set of notes without proceeding to make a final summary.

It is usually advisable to work in paragraphs and to reproduce the paragraphing of the original in your summary. This makes sense because each paragraph in the original (assuming it is a well written piece!) will deal with one aspect of the discussion and this pattern will be reflected in your summary. From time to time you will find paragraphs that contain only a sentence or two of essential material. It would then be up to you to decide if they might be combined into one paragraph in your shortened version. For the most part, however, it is best to keep to the paragraphing of the original.

3 What is essential? The whole art of summarizing depends on how you answer this question – and summarizing is an art! Therefore a good deal depends on your own judgement. As often happens when you write, you should put yourself in the position of the person who is to read the summary. If you omit a certain point, will his or her understanding of the argument be hindered? Perhaps you yourself, as a student, will want to read that summary in a year's time for exam revision. Will you be able to follow the argument without that link? If you consider that the reader – another person or yourself – can do without the point, then your decision is made: the sentence is not essential.

Illustrations and examples used by the original writer to enhance his arguments are another problem for the summarizer. Some would say that all examples are expendable, since they do not add anything to the argument, but only present it in another way. On the other hand, a well-chosen example can bring the whole discussion to life and change an arid piece of abstract writing into something vivid and understandable. Therefore consider each example on its merits. You may well be able to dispense with most of them, but from time to time an effective example will be well worth its place in your summary.

4 When you have worked through the paragraphs, as described above, you will be left with a list of main points written out in

complete sentences. You are now in a position to write your summary. *In fact the first draft of your summary is already in front of you!* This is the important reason for using complete sentences which we hinted at in section 2 above. You have no need to 'write up' the notes you have taken. The listed points, following from one to the next, are already a draft for you to work on. All you have to do is to make sure that each group of sentences moves smoothly together as a paragraph. For this purpose, you may have to supply link words and phrases such as 'therefore', 'however', 'on the other hand' or merely 'and' and 'but'. You would also revise, where necessary, the wording of your sentences to make sure they are expressed as well as possible. If for any reason you have to work to a word limit, you can count the words at this stage and make any necessary modifications. Once you are satisfied, you can write or type out your final version without any further intermediate stage.

To illustrate this technique, we will make a summary of the following passage of 407 words about the early twentieth-century soap manufacturer, Lord Leverhulme:

> The euphoric madness that burst out in Britain after the war shook the commercial worlds of fashion and entertainment. Near insatiable consumer demand after wartime deprivation encouraged the growth of all kinds of business, and wartime profits were available to finance expansion and new ventures. Released from discipline and restriction, and free at last from the fear of sudden death, most people were hell-bent on returning to the things they had done before the war; when they did so they intended to pursue them without pre-war inhibitions. Leverhulme was no exception, save perhaps for the scale of his imprudence. He had unfinished business left over from before the war — left over, indeed, from 1906. He wanted control of those soap firms that had so far evaded the Lever Brothers' net; Crossfield's, Gossage's, Knight's and some smaller firms — everything except the powerful and untouchable C.W.S. By 1920 these last citadels of the private soap industry were his, and he controlled nearly two-thirds of British production. It was a development which attracted the attention of the Beveridge Committee on Trusts, and a Government enquiry on the costs and profits of Lever Brothers' operations eventually decided that the price of household soap must be reduced by twopence, to ninepence a pound. Leverhulme had argued his case pointing to the great cost and complexity of his Company's activities beyond the simple making

and selling of soap, but the committee was not prepared to take the view that soap prices should support tropical ventures no matter how great their promise of commercial, or even political, benefits in the long run.

To buy out the remainder of the private soap industry, and thereby settle some old scores, Leverhulme paid a very high price. He had in nearly every case made the directors of the companies he took over an offer which was 'too good to refuse'. Leverhulme was dedicated to the practice of business and not to its cash rewards, and he had always believed that the business drive of the less totally dedicated was vulnerable to monetary considerations. He believed that Ordinary shareholders, content with a good dividend and unwilling to jeopardise it, would resist promising but risky business ventures. For this reason he had kept the Ordinary shares in his own hands and issued Preference shares, with fixed dividends, to the public. He was applying the same principle when he persuaded his competitors to exchange their business interests for his cash.

(from *Lord Leverhulme* by W. P. Jolly, Constable Publishers, 1976)

The listed points derived from this passage are:

Paragraph one

1 After the war there was rapid business expansion, financed by wartime profits.
2 Released from fear and inhibitions, most people were eager to pursue their pre-war activities.
3 Leverhulme was among them.
4 He wanted to finish his pre-war attempts to take control of all the other soap firms, except C.W.S. which was too powerful.
5 By 1920 he had gained control of nearly two-thirds of British soap production.
6 This led to a Government inquiry into Leverhulme's costs and profits.
7 The Government ordered the price of household soap to be cut by twopence, to ninepence a pound.
8 Leverhulme had argued that his company had many more activities than making and selling soap.
9 The committee was not impressed.
10 It did not think soap prices should finance the company's

ventures in the tropics despite long-term business and even political benefits.

Paragraph two

11 Acquiring the private soap industry cost Leverhulme dearly, since he had to pay the outgoing directors sums 'too good to refuse'.

12 Since owners of Ordinary shares might be unwilling to support risky adventures, he retained these himself and only issued Preference shares with a fixed interest.

13 He was applying this same principle to his competitors when he persuaded them to sell their business interest for cash.

If you read through these numbered points you will see that we already have the first draft of a summary. At present it lacks links between some of the points. We have to supply 'and' between 2 and 3; 'but' between 5 and 6; 'as a result' between 6 and 7, and 'despite the fact that' between 7 and 8. This is also the time to reconsider the phrasing and make any desirable changes. If you are limited to a prescribed number of words (as in an examination, for instance), you can count the words in this draft and if you have exceeded your limit you can look over the points and see if any more can be dispensed with. The original passage is 407 words long and the outline above, together with the links, would make just over 200. There is a tradition that summaries should be about one-third of the original. Should you feel it necessary to reduce your first draft by another fifty or seventy words, you could look at points 12 and 13 again. On reflection, you may decide that they do not add a great deal to our understanding of Leverhulme's acquisition of the soap industry and could be omitted. Points 9 and 10 might also be left out if it was essential to reduce the word count. You will notice that all these important decisions are taken before you move from your set of notes. You can do this because you wrote the notes out in complete sentences in the first place. Now you can write out the final version:

After the war there was a rapid business expansion, financed by wartime profits. Released from fear and inhibitions, most people were eager to pursue their pre-war activities and Leverhulme was among them. He wanted to finish his pre-war attempts to take control of all the other soap firms, except C.W.S. which was too powerful. By 1920 he had gained control of nearly two-thirds of British soap production, but this led to a Government inquiry into Leverhulme's costs and profits. As a result, the Government ordered that the price of household soap be reduced by twopence, to ninepence a pound, despite the fact that Leverhulme argued that his company had many more activities than making and selling soap. Acquiring the private soap industry cost Leverhulme dearly, since he had to pay the outgoing directors sums 'too good to refuse'.

(138 words)

Summary

Familiarize yourself with the material as a whole.

Paragraph by paragraph, select the essential points of the argument.

Write these down *as complete sentences*. This at once provides you with a first draft.

Insert the necessary sentence links.

Check the number of words used and revise the draft if you are over a permitted limit.

Make a fair copy.

8 Reports

A report answers a question!

This is the principle that underlies all report writing. Keep this idea firmly in your mind throughout the many activities that lead to the finished product and you have every prospect of presenting a successful report. Lose sight of this principle and your report will miss its mark.

The usual reason for writing a report is that some person or some organization needs information on a problem and answers are wanted to one or more questions posed by that situation. The report writer has to gather the necessary evidence, select and arrange it in the most effective order, set it out in words that can be understood by the readers, draw conclusions from it and (if asked to do so) make recommendations. The desired result is an answer to the question that first prompted the inquiry.

When one thinks of bulky government reports, sometimes hundreds of pages long, the prospect of writing a report may seem alarming. But reports can be quite short. Sometimes a report of only a few pages will admirably fulfil the requirements of the person commissioning it.

Many of us have the experience of writing short reports. One of the commonest, unhappily, is the vehicle accident report in an insurance claim. To be certain that the necessary evidence is given efficiently, insurance companies produce forms which ask specific questions: details of the cars and drivers involved, makes of the cars, time and place of the incident, weather conditions and so on. Then there is a space for a written report in which we can explain in our own words exactly what happened. Such forms also include an item which is relevant to many bigger and more formal reports – namely, a diagram. On the insurance claim form it will be used to show the relative positions of the vehicles and points of impact. In many technical reports, diagrams and charts will have an important part to play reinforcing the written text.

The main features of an insurance form are typical of all good report writing – well-structured presentation of evidence, avoiding all that is irrelevant and concentrating only on what may affect the conclusions; graphic material to clarify the written word and written evidence presented in a succinct and objective manner. Because an insurance company has prepared the form for its own use, it completely fulfils the important requirement that a report should be designed specifically for the person who is to read it and make decisions from it.

Other reports commonly in use and based on structures well understood by those who write them and those who read them include reports by the police, fire officers, surveyors of property, doctors and teachers. School reports have a very special place in most people's memories! The growth of pupil profiles, as well as reports for employers and those on UCCA forms for university applications, makes this a branch of report-writing that requires skill and sensitivity. It is also very time consuming for the teachers who have to do it.

In commerce, industry and government, report writers do not have printed forms to rely on. They have to structure their reports themselves and it is here that skills in clear English are brought into play, together with an understanding of how such reports should be prepared and presented.

We want a report on . . .

If someone says this to you, you may be elated at being given the responsibility or daunted by the challenge. Before you decide which emotion is appropriate, you require the fundamental information on which the whole exercise will be based: what are the terms of reference? This is another way of stating what has been said at the beginning of this chapter: what is the question being asked?

Reports are initiated because someone sees a problem. In public life it may be a large-scale catastrophe such as a rail crash or a mine disaster. There may be great concern over a threat to the environment. Such inquiries would answer questions about how the accident had happened and how a similar incident could be prevented in the future. Within a business, the questions may be about relocating a factory, developing new markets or new products, or about ways of combating petty pilfering! In every case, hard evidence is needed and conclusions must be drawn that answer the questions and enable those in authority to take decisions. Therefore at the beginning of the report-writing process you must know exactly what you are being asked to do. These instructions will be your terms of reference.

As an example, let's assume that you work for a charitable organization that has been given a substantial sum of money to build a community hall in a small country town. The need for the hall is well known; the money is now available and your organization has been offered three possible sites. You are asked to write a report on the suitability of each site and make a recommendation. Your terms of reference might read as follows: to investigate the suitability of the sites at Mill Lane, Orchard Park and Tucker's Field for the construction of a community hall and to make a recommendation as to which site should be chosen.

You will notice that in these terms of reference you are asked specifically to make a recommendation. This will not always be so. Management may wish to consider the evidence you are presenting (and which you sum up in your conclusion) and then make their own decision. In any case, even if you are asked to make a recommendation, it will not necessarily be acted on.

Who is to read it?

Once you have digested your terms of reference, you have to consider the person or group of people who will read the report. You will be writing specifically for this readership and what you know about your readers will influence your style. For instance, the evidence you present may be of a highly technical nature and this will be easier to write if you are able to use technical terms that only professionals in this area will understand. The person who has commissioned the report may be quite at home with the technical language and will have no difficulty following it. On the other hand he may be the managing director of a large organization with many varied interests and he may be unfamiliar with the technical language of your particular subdivision. You will therefore have to write your report in such a way that these technical matters can be understood by someone who is not an expert and yet has to make the final decisions. Your report may also be circulated to a number of people who will contribute to the decision making or who will be affected by it. Some may be technically expert while others may not. Your manner of writing will have to take account of both kinds of reader.

Yet another consideration is whether or not your report is to be published. If it is, then you will be writing for a general readership and you will not be able to assume that every reader is familiar with the internal working of your organization nor with the technicalities you are discussing.

Why, when and how much . . .?

You must know the answers to these three questions before you embark on collecting evidence for your report. The answer to why the report has been asked for should already be obvious from your terms of reference. If clarification is called for, this is the time to seek it. You must be fully aware of the situation that has prompted the report and the possible decisions that may be taken as a result of it.

The question, 'when?' is a thoroughly practical one. You must find out how long you have to prepare the report. If you are expected to put the report into the hands of the readers in an unreasonably short time, you may be able to negotiate a more suitable date or ask for more assistance and resources.

This leads to the question, 'how much?' The cost of a major report will be considerable and even a quite modest one will require resources. It is as well to be sure at the outset that you will be allowed whatever is necessary in money and support. The latter may include secretarial assistance, graphics and reprographics, typing or printing, binding and eventually the circulation of the report.

'How much?' may also be applied to the quantity of the report, better expressed as, 'how long?' There is no set length to a report. Some run to hundreds of pages; others deal with the matter in a dozen or so. Length will depend on the nature and complexity of the terms of reference and the amount of evidence to be considered. The most effective reports are often among the shortest. Provided that no essential evidence and information is left out, there is everything to be said for a report that is easy to assimilate in one reading.

Gathering the evidence . . .

A report is not a set of personal reflections on the matter under review. It is an impersonal collection of evidence relevant to the subject, selected, arranged and presented effectively, with conclusions drawn and recommendations made (if these have been asked for). The kind of evidence and its sources will depend on the nature of the inquiry, but it is likely to involve research into written material and personal interviews. If we consider the example suggested above of a report on the suitability of three sites on which to build a community hall, we can see that it may be necessary to study other reports on development plans for the town, papers on the preservation of the local environment, even the history of each site as well as rival plans for the utilization of these areas. You will also want to take evidence from a number of interested parties – site owners, planning officials, neighbours whose own properties may be affected by the development, local history and environmental groups and so on. Skill is required in sifting through all this evidence and selecting what will have a bearing on the choice of a site and the possibility of acquiring it without running into difficulties.

Once the evidence, written and spoken, has been collected, it must be recorded and filed in a systematic way. Evidence will come to hand from various sources and the researcher must have a system to deal with it. Some use cards which can be catalogued and filed under different headings. Others use loose-leaf files in which papers can be rearranged or added to as the necessity arises. Another method is to build up a set of notebooks – one for each aspect of the evidence. The important thing is to bring as quickly as you can the evidence you have gathered into the safety of a permanent 'bank' and not leave an untidy mass of papers to be sorted out 'later on'. When the time comes, some vital detail may have been lost among the jottings. If material is stored on a computer, then the discs should be copied frequently in case of an accident to the originals.

Verbal evidence

Most reports will make use of information given in interviews to the researcher. Great skill is needed to elicit what is really useful and to distinguish objective evidence from hearsay and personal opinion. Researchers should be quite certain in their own minds what they wish to discover from the person being interviewed. It is a good policy to prepare in advance the questions you wish to ask, although you should always be prepared for the unexpected remark that may yield something useful but totally unforeseen. Take care not to intimidate your interviewee with too obvious attempts to write down everything that is said. If you wish to tape record the interview, you may have to prepare the ground very carefully, making sure that a microphone does not inhibit the person whose help you are seeking. Remember too that almost everybody from whom you obtain evidence is likely to have an interest in the results of your report. People will tend to angle the evidence towards whatever seems to them to be a desirable outcome.

When you have gathered the evidence from individuals, you will have to evaluate it, bearing in mind this personal element. For example, someone may present you with evidence that building your hall on one of the sites would be an environmental disaster. The fact that he owns a house on the edge of the site will obviously affect the way you evaluate his evidence! Again, a person without official status but possessed of local knowledge going back a great many years may have observations that are well worth balancing against views of official planners who have their own ideas about the site but who live and work far away from the town.

Preparing to write . . .

Once you have gathered the evidence, you must decide the manner in which it is to be presented. You will select headings appropriate to the inquiry you are conducting and group the evidence under them so that each aspect of the subject can be assessed in turn. Your report on sites for the community hall might be divided into sections dealing with the present ownership, location and access, legal aspects and planning permission, environmental considerations, financial constraints, surveyors' reports and so on.

When you have settled upon the structure and its component sections, you then have to consider how much of the evidence to include. Obviously you are not going to suppress important evidence, but you may well have to select what is of major importance and leave out other material which says much the same thing, or else relegate it to an appendix. Too much detail can clog up a report: too little will make it appear superficial.

The section of the report likely to cause the greatest interest is the one giving your conclusions. These will have been growing in your mind as you gathered the evidence, but until all the evidence is before you, no conclusion can be reached with complete confidence. Something uncovered at the very end of the investigation may throw quite a different light on the question.

When you draw your conclusions, they may or may not be what was expected (or desired) but you have to state your view honestly and as objectively as possible. Your conclusions may include specific recommendations. Whether these are to be acted on or ignored is not your decision and the success or failure of your report does not depend upon it – whatever your personal feelings. The report will have succeeded if it has presented the necessary evidence in a readable manner, evaluating it and reaching an objective conclusion so that a convincing answer has been given to the question which initiated the whole process.

The layout of a report

There is no hard and fast rule about how a report should be laid out, but a pattern has emerged from general usage which can serve as a basis for most reports:

A title page
Terms of reference
Table of Contents
Summary
Body of the report
Conclusions
Appendices

The first item on the list speaks for itself, but it reminds us that the whole appearance of the report is important. Introduced by a well-designed title page, perfectly typed and attractively laid out, the report, by its very appearance, should encourage people to read it. It is off-putting to be presented with many pages of closely packed print with little to guide the reader from one section to another. That is why you must make a decision about headings, subheadings and the numbering of the paragraphs. Each main section should begin on a fresh page under a bold heading. If we assume that your report is to be typed, rather than printed, your typist should be asked to use the resources of upper-case letters, underlining and extra spacing to highlight both headings and subheadings. If the report is to be printed, then you should consult with the printer about achieving the best effect.

The terms of reference will provide you with the title of the report, although if they are wordy you could devise a brief title as a heading and then follow it with the terms of reference, fully set out, beneath.

You will naturally have taken a decision about the numbering of the pages and paragraphs before you compile the Table of Contents. Within the report you may wish to refer forwards and backwards to other material; those who will discuss the report will want an easy system of reference to locate relevant items within it. One method is to number the pages and also each paragraph within a chapter. Thus something in the fifth paragraph of chapter seven can easily be found if the reader is referred to 7.5. Another way is to number every paragraph consecutively from the beginning of the report to the end. This does away with the necessity for page numbers (though they can be included and would be useful for turning to the start of each chapter). On the other hand, the consecutive numbering of paragraphs can lead in a long report to very high numbers. The chapter and paragraph method is probably preferable.

Placing the summary at the beginning of the report may seem surprising, but the reason for this is to enable the reader to understand the scope of the report, the method employed and its principle conclusions. Within an organization there will be some people who are too busy to study the report at length, or whose interest is limited to an awareness of its conclusions. For them, the summary is all they wish to read and it is placed at the beginning so that they can turn to it immediately. Some report writers prefer to place the summary at the end, which would seem to be a logical place for it. In any event you would write it after you had composed the main body of the report. Whether you place it eventually at the beginning or the end is your decision.

You will have given considerable thought to the presentation of the body of the report. It is essential to have a well-considered structure. From the mass of evidence gained from research into documents, possibly from experiments and tests, and certainly from interviews, you have to produce shape and coherence. In some reports you will be tracing a series of events and a chronological structure will suggest itself. Our example of choosing the site for a community hall would draw evidence from a number of different interests and approaches, each having reference to the three different locations. You would make up your mind whether it would be more effective to have three main divisions – one for each site – and under each one deal with the sections on planning, finance, environmental factors and so on, or alternatively to use planning, finance and environmental factors as main headings and under these consider each site in turn.

When you are quite convinced that you have the best structure for your purposes, you can move on to your detailed planning. Start by preparing an outline of the report. This is for you to work from and will not be printed as part of the report. Planning in this way will allow you to decide what evidence to include and the order in which to present it. This is not a decision you can leave until you begin writing the first draft.

Unlike so many other forms of writing, the first draft of a report is not going to be your first opportunity to sort out your thoughts through the very act of writing. Gathering the evidence, writing it up in your files or notebooks, drawing up a plan for the report – in all these activities you will already have done a good deal of thinking, so that by the time you come to write the main body of the report you should be expressing what has already been sorted out in your mind. You are familiar wth the evidence and know your conclusions.

Naturally, you will find that there are moments when the right words seem to elude you. This may be a symptom of some uncertainty still remaining in your mind. You will overcome the obstacle and move on as soon as you know exactly what you think or wish to say about this particular point. For the most part, however, your first draft should come without too much difficulty because you have already done so much preliminary work.

On completion of the first draft, it may be as well to put it aside for a day or two (if time permits) before returning to it with a fresh eye. Keep in view all the time the questions you set out to answer and make sure that the evidence you have selected and the conclusions you have reached deal with them adequately.

A second opinion is always valuable. Before you make the final draft, you may be able to pass the report to two or three trusted colleagues to find out their reactions. Praise would be heart-warming, but precise suggestions about where and how the report could be improved would be more useful. You would not expect to go back and rewrite the report completely, but the opinion of someone who comes to the report with a fresh eye may direct you to a few places where you could make improvements. Perhaps more detail is needed to make a piece of evidence effective. Far more likely is the request for less detail. The reader only wants the essential information, and if a point has already been made quite adequately there is no need to dwell on it or repeat it.

Your own careful revision of the first draft will precede the final version. (You hope there is no need for a second or third draft before the final one!) This is the manuscript or typescript that will be passed to the typist or printer and you must therefore set it out exactly as you want it, with the headings and subheadings which you have decided to use and the paragraphs numbered.

The report may conclude with appendices containing additional material that was not required in the main body of the text. In this section it is courteous to acknowledge those who have in any way assisted you. After proof-correcting and whatever binding is deemed necessary, the report is ready for presentation to those who have commissioned it. You have compiled the evidence, reached conclusions and perhaps you have made recommendations. The decisions are in the hands of others.

Throughout this section, it has been assumed that the report is the work of one person. Quite often a committee is set up to make the report. The methods outlined above still apply and the actual writing of the report is likely to devolve on one person. However, there are bound to be some modifications to the process. For example, the first draft would have to be circulated to all the members for their approval and the views of those who disagreed with the conclusions of the majority would have to be expressed in a minority report.

Style in reports

The key word is objectivity. A report sets out to establish the truth of a situation and to find honest answers to the questions which have been raised. Hard facts and firm evidence are required and therefore an informal, personal tone is out of place. This does not mean that the use of such words as 'I' or 'we' is completely ruled out. It does mean, however, that they are used in a judicious manner to express a considered opinion and not an emotional response.

Since the point of any report is to make information readily accessible to the reader (who may not be an expert in the subject) every effort must be made to write *clear English* and the advice contained elsewhere in this book applies. A readily understood vocabulary and a preference for short rather than long sentences is a good basis for report writing. The use of technical terms depends on how well they are understood by those who will read the report. If laymen have to make policy decisions on a scientific or technological matter, then the report must either avoid technical terms or explain them. The writer must resist the temptation to give his report a false air of importance by using long words and inflated language. He or she will earn much more praise for writing which is easy to understand, objective and to the point.

A whole book devoted to this topic is *Report Writing* by Doris Wheatley (Penguin, 1988).

Summary

A report answers a question.

It should be a well-structured presentation of evidence with conclusions drawn from it.

Be quite certain what is required of your report (i.e. what the terms of reference are).

Always have in mind who is to read your report.

At the start of your work you should know by what date the report is required and what resources you have at your disposal.

A short report may be more effective than a very long one.

File the evidence you gather systematically so that retrieval is easy.

The structure of your report is important. Plan it carefully.

Your conclusions must be honest and objective. They must answer the question(s) which the report sets out to consider.

9 The Minutes

A special kind of report writing is the compiling of the minutes of a meeting. The minutes are a factual account of its transactions and they become its permanent and official record. It is the duty of the secretary of an organization to take the minutes, noting down details of the discussions and then the decisions arrived at. The minutes are not a transcript of absolutely everything that is said, but a fair summary of the main points of every significant contribution and a completely accurate statement of what is proposed (and by whom), what amendments are tabled and the outcome of the voting.

Every properly constituted organization, however small, should have the minutes of its proceedings taken down and subsequently written in the minute book. This is particularly necessary if funds are involved and decisions are taken by a committee on behalf of members who are not present. The accuracy of the secretary's work is checked when the meeting next convenes. Then the secretary has to read aloud the minutes of the previous meeting before new business is discussed. This enables members who were present at the previous meeting to assure themselves that it was correctly minuted and to propose any necessary corrections. Then a vote is taken on whether or not to accept the minutes as 'a true and accurate record' (to use a traditional phrase). Once the minutes have been accepted, they are regarded as the official record of that meeting.

Some organizations arrange for the minutes to be typed and duplicated and sent out to members well in advance of the next meeting. This gives members time to study what has been written and to note any possible inaccuracies. It also saves time at the meeting because there is no need for the secretary to read the minutes aloud, provided that the chairman allows a short time for any corrections to be made.

The form of the minutes should follow the agenda of the meeting. Usually this begins with the chairman reading out the names of those who have sent apologies for absence. Next comes the reading of the minutes and their acceptance. Time is then given to the discussion of any matter arising from the minutes. This would come about if a member had undertaken at the previous meeting to do something on behalf of the committee or to find out some information. He or she could report back at this stage. After this any correspondence that has been received is reported and discussed, as necessary. Then new business is introduced, either for discussion or in the form of proposals to be voted on. Towards the end of the meeting, there is a slot for 'Any Other Business' – that is to say, business which arose too late for inclusion in the official agenda. Finally, the date, time and place of the next meeting are decided on. An agenda would therefore look like this:

1 Apologies for absence
2 The minutes of the previous meeting
3 Matters arising
4 Correspondence
5 (New business)
6 etc.
7 etc.
8 etc.
9 Any other business
10 Date of the next meeting

Style

It is usual for minutes to be written in an impersonal style. A secretary would not begin, 'We all met at John's house last week . . .' He or she would phrase it more formally as, 'A meeting of the committee was held at the house of Mr John Smith on 24 January 1989, commencing at 7.45 p.m. There were seven members present.' The minutes would continue in this formal style, reporting the ebb and flow of the meeting. Strong feelings might be expressed, but the secretary would maintain the objective manner and take care not to allow his or her own feelings to intrude into this official record.

Reported speech

The writing of minutes is to do with reporting what people have said without actually quoting them! This requires the skill known as 'reported speech'. Another name for it is 'indirect speech', though the first term describes what is being done more precisely. Suppose this remark was made in a public speech: 'I am telling you that this government has no idea what to do about unemployment. It had no policy when it came to office and it has no policy now. It should have resigned months ago.' This sentiment could be re-expressed with far less impact but with a greater degree of formality as follows: Mr — said that he was telling his audience that the government had no idea what to do about unemployment. It had had no policy when it came to office and it had no policy at the present time. It should have resigned months before. Not a very exciting statement! The version in direct speech, that is, quoting the actual words of the speaker, is far more telling.

All the same, there are many occasions when it is convenient to use reported speech. For instance, such a version enables the writer to get to the heart of what is being said, cutting out rhetorical phrases and presenting a summary of the main points of the remarks. The politician's sentence, quoted above, might be reported in the local paper as: 'Mr — said that the government had no policy on unemployment and never had one. Its resignation was long overdue.'

Reported speech is normally used when writing up the minutes of a meeting. This avoids the necessity of recording the precise words of a speaker (very difficult if you are not a shorthand writer!). It also allows the secretary to select the main points from all that a speaker has said. What is more, the use of indirect speech in the minutes places every contribution on the same level of factual reporting.

There are certain rules to be followed when changing a passage from direct to indirect (reported) speech. The rigid application of these rules will sometimes render the new version stilted or even obscure. As always, the writer must use his or her judgement and modify anything that makes the text awkward or unpleasing. Before you modify the rules, however, it is as well to understand them.

Here is a summary of the changes necessary when moving from direct to indirect speech:

1 Verbs move back one tense. That is to say, a verb in the present tense (e.g. *speak*) moves into the past tense (e.g. *spoke*) and one already in the past moves further back into the past to a tense which some grammarians call the pluperfect (e.g. *had spoken*).

2 All pronouns in the first and second person (e.g. I, me, we, us, you) become third person (e.g. he, him, she, her, they, them), for example:

   (a) direct speech: The mayor said, 'I regard you as a hero. You risked your life for the child. I shall never forget what you have done.'

   (b) indirect (reported) speech: The mayor said that he regarded him as a hero. He had risked his life for the child. He would never forget what he had done.

You can see immediately one problem with the strict application of the rules of reported speech. In the third sentence of (b) the word 'he' is used twice and it is not clear whether it is the mayor or the hero who will never forget what he had done. This difficulty can be overcome by replacing the first 'he' with 'the mayor' and the second 'he' with 'the fireman'. The sentence would then read: The mayor would never forget what the fireman had done.

As you apply Rules 1 and 2 above, other things follow logically from them. Since reported speech is telling of something that has already happened and is now over and done with, words which refer to the present time must be changed to those appropriate to reporting events in the past: e.g. 'here' becomes 'there'; 'this' becomes 'that'; 'these' become 'those'; 'now' becomes 'then'; 'ago' becomes 'before'; 'today' becomes 'that day'; 'yesterday' becomes 'the day before' (or 'the previous day'); 'tomorrow' becomes 'the day after' (or 'the next day').

Note too that 'may' becomes 'might'; 'will' becomes 'would'; 'shall' becomes 'should'; 'can' becomes 'could'.

The following short passages will illustrate the changes that are necessary when using only reported speech. Passage (a) is in direct speech and is quoting the actual words of the Entertainments Officer;

in passage (b) the remarks of the Entertainments Officer are not quoted as he spoke them but are given as reported speech:

> (a) Answering questions from the visiting tour operators, the Entertainments Officer said, 'My county has every amenity a holiday-maker can wish for. Ten years ago it was different: we had no swimming pool and no sports facilities worth talking about. Yet here you can see for yourselves what my department has achieved in the building of this leisure complex. When you visit the coast tomorrow, I will show you what my colleagues and I are planning for the children and what may be in store for water-sports enthusiasts.'

> (b) Answering questions from visiting tour operators, the Entertainments Officer said that his county had every amenity a holiday-maker could wish for. Ten years before it had been different. They had had no swimming pool and no sports facilities worth talking about. Yet there the tour operators could see for themselves what his department had achieved in the building of that leisure complex. When they visited the coast the next day, he would show them what he and his colleagues were planning for the children and what might be in store for water-sports enthusiasts.

Using reported speech correctly is very much a matter of common sense and of following what sounds right. Once you have begun with a phrase such as, 'He said that . .' or 'She replied that . . .', keep in mind that you are taking words spoken in what was the *present* time as far as the speaker was concerned and are reporting them as remarks which were made some time in the *past*.

Summary

The minutes of a meeting provide a factual account of the transactions that took place. They summarize the main points of the discussion and record the decisions taken.

The style is impersonal.

Reported (or indirect) speech records what a speaker has said without directly quoting the words he used. Quotation marks therefore are not needed.

To change direct speech to reported speech, move the verbs back a tense into the past and change all first and second person pronouns to the third person. Words referring to the present time must be changed to those appropriate to the past.

10 Answering Essay Questions

'For this week's assignment, I want you to write an essay on . . .' The title falls gently from the tutor's lips and the student scribbles it down on his pad of file paper, relaxed in the knowledge that the essay is tomorrow's problem. But when the morrow comes, the task of writing the essay confronts him. Where to find the material – how to organize it – what does the title really mean – how much am I expected to write – do I need an introduction – and how do I begin? Questions crowd in upon him and he wishes the tutor had taken as much trouble to teach him to write an essay as to impart the matter of the lesson. It is an unfortunate fact of academic life that too many teachers assume that their students know how to write essays, although evidence to the contrary arrives on their desks every Monday morning.

Essay writing is one of the most regular tasks to face students, whether they are in full-time education, on part-time training, attending evening classes or studying at home by means of correspondence courses. It is a prime learning tool because it forces the student to organize what he has been taught and apply it to the question or topic set out in the title. The student may have pages and pages of notes but these are of little value unless the knowledge can be applied flexibly to a given problem. The learning gained in the classroom and library must be filtered through the student's mind as he selects, interprets and comments on material relevant to the matter in hand. In this way he makes the knowledge his own.

The essay not only teaches; it also tests. Whether you, as a student, face a three-hour paper or have to submit a file of course work, your essays will decide the result of your examination. Now that continuous assessment is well established as an alternative to a 'sudden death' examination, every essay you write may contribute to your final grade. However good your knowledge, an inability to express it adequately in the form of an essay will be a severe handicap to your progress in education and training.

Good teachers (who these days may also be assessors) will take pains to teach their students how they expect essays to be written and presented. There will be differences in technique for different subjects. For example, scientific essays will include calculations, formulae, blocks of data, etc. A subject such as Geography will call for the drawing of maps; technical subjects will require diagrams, and in literary subjects quotations from authors and critics will be essential. Yet, allowing for such differences, there still remains much that all essays have in common. In this section we will try to answer the heart-cry of the inexperienced student who, uninstructed in essay writing and faced with the necessity of writing a thousand words on a given topic, groans, 'I don't know how to begin!'

Why am I doing this . . .?

Be clear about the reasons for writing your essay. The purpose is twofold; (a) to assist your learning by making you apply what you have been taught to a particular problem and (b) to show the teacher – or examiner – how much you have learned and how effectively you can use it. A successful essay will supply the answer to a question on the basis of sound knowledge and its intelligent, thoughtful application. There are thus two elements: the factual information and the use made of it.

The factual information that will underpin your essay will be in the notes you have taken at lectures or during your private study. Often an essay title will be designed to extend your knowledge by making you take your reading into areas of the subject that are new to you. If this is so, then you begin the essay writing process by further research, adding to your general store of notes at the same time as you seek out material specifically for the essay. When you have completed this task, you are in a position to look over the material you have gathered and *think about it!*

Students are often in too much of a hurry to begin. Time for thought is essential for there is plenty to think about.

What am I being asked?

Essay titles can be several sentences long (e.g. a quotation set for your comments) or as brief as 'Was John Donne a great poet?' Whatever form the title takes, you must be sure that you know exactly what it means – and what may lie behind it. That question about John Donne seems obvious enough: there is no difficulty in understanding the wording. But why has anyone bothered to ask it about such a famous poet? Behind the question is the implication that some people have doubted his greatness. What were their reasons; how valid do you think they are; do you yourself have reservations about this poet's reputation? This is the matter of your essay and you cannot plan your answer until you have thought carefully about what you are being asked.

With a long title, it is easy to pick out one key phrase and assume that is all you have to consider. You could be very wrong indeed. Go through the title like a lawyer, weighing the significance of every word until you are confident you understand the question. It might help to underline key words and phrases – provided you do not mistake one phrase for the whole title!

How am I going to treat this topic?

Often this question answers itself as soon as you have fully understood the question. But there are many occasions when a title will be capable of various interpretations – all of them valid. This means that you must decide which aspect you propose to write about, and near the beginning of the essay you must explain how you understand the title and how you propose to explore it. At this stage it may be necessary to define some terms used in the title, showing how you interpret them. For example, that title mentioned above, 'Was John Donne a great poet?' begs the question as to what is meant by a 'great poet', and it might be necessary to define the qualities of poetic greatness before you consider the works of John Donne himself.

Have I sufficient knowledge?

This may seem an odd question to ask yourself at this stage, but it is intended to make you think about the background of information on which you will base your opinions. It is possible that your essay may be a straightforward exercise in factual recall and nothing else.

But most essays in higher education ask for your reaction to a discussion point; your solution to a problem; your views on the application of a technique to a given situation. The satisfactory answers will be those that are founded on adequate knowledge of the subject, well displayed in the essay. A damning criticism is the word 'thin' – implying that the writer's arguments are of little value because they are based on too limited a range of evidence and show ignorance of much that is important to the discussion. It is therefore essential at the very outset to re-study the topic, looking up relevant notes, re-reading passages of text and, if necessary, widening your research.

How do I begin?

You have understood the title and defined its terms; you have brought to mind the knowledge on which your essay will be based and you have decided on your approach. These are the important preliminaries. How do you move on to putting words on paper?

With an eye firmly on the essay title, jot down as many relevant ideas, facts, figures, references and examples as you can. This is the brain-storming process intended to gather together the material on which you will build your essay. The entries will be quite short. It is possible that one phrase will serve as shorthand for a whole block of information or opinion. This may find itself side by side with a random idea that will prove to be of no importance at all. The object is to get your mind working on the question to the extent of writing things down.

After that first flurry of ideas, you may be impressed by the richness of what you have written. More probably you will be dismayed at the lack of ideas and the shallowness of your supporting evidence. This is not a moment for despair – only for hard thought. Take each jotted note in turn and try to make each one suggest another idea to you. Look again at your file of notes or, in a literary subject, at the text you are studying. Have you overlooked valuable discussion points? Think again of the essay title. Challenge yourself to find something in it to add to your list of ideas.

Planning the essay

The shape of an essay may leap to your mind in the very moment of reading the title. Sometimes it will grow on you as you research your material and find ways into the topic. Yet again, there will be occasions when the structure will remain undecided until you have gone through the brain-storming process and are able to contemplate the evidence and arguments you have brought together in your jottings. This is the latest you can leave it. Now there must be decisions about the form your essay is to take.

The jotted notes contain all the ideas you have been able to bring together on the subject. You must now find the ones truly relevant to the title, grouping together those that reinforce each other and discarding those that you will be unable to use after all. If your brain-storming scattered useful points widely across your paper, it will be a good idea to rewrite the list of notes, bringing them into better order and removing those that are not needed. This process of sifting and rearranging is a necessary preliminary to making an essay plan.

Some students dislike planning too much in advance, preferring to begin writing and letting one idea lead to the next and so on until a conclusion is reached. If the final result is satisfactory, there can be no complaint about this method, but it is a dangerous one for the inexperienced writer. A predetermined plan provides a structure that keeps a writer to the point, deters him from wandering off the subject and discourages any tendency to unbalance the essay by dwelling too long on one point. What is more, it compels the writer to think out his argument before putting pen to paper.

Essentially an essay plan is a list of paragraph headings. By defini-tion, a paragraph deals with a single aspect of the subject or one particular step in the argument. Somewhere within it will be a sen-tence that enshrines the key idea of the paragraph. (Some people call this the 'topic sentence'.) Your essay plan will be a list of these topic sentences arranged in the order in which you propose to use them. If you find it helpful, you can jot down under each topic sentence supporting ideas, examples, references, etc. to use within the paragraph. This kind of plan is, in effect, an outline of the essay. If it has been carefully and thoughtfully put together, the task of writing the essay has been made much easier, because so many decisions will already have been made. Without such a plan, the writer must pause at each new paragraph to think of the way forward – the next step in the argument and the material to support it. With a good plan, this has already been done and the writer can concentrate on the act of writing as he fleshes out the bare bones of the plan.

The beginning . . .

The opening of an essay deserves special consideration. The first sentence or two should catch the attention of the reader, encouraging him to read on. It may be a provocative remark, an apt quotation from an acknowledged expert or even a briefly told illustration of the problem to be considered. Then the writer must set out his stall – that is, explain how he understands the question and how he proposes to treat it, defining any terms whose meaning may be arguable. Here is an essay title to do with Jane Austen's novel, *Pride and Prejudice*:

> The author began by calling her book 'First Impressions' but later changed it to 'Pride and Prejudice'. Which do you think is the better title?

The essay might begin as follows:

> Publishers encourage authors to choose titles to catch the eye and sell books. Their relation to what the books are about is a secondary matter. Jane Austen's first choice for her famous novel was 'First Impressions'. It was many years later (for the book was a long time in the writing) that, encouraged by her publisher, she changed the title to 'Pride and Prejudice'.
>
> Was she right to do so? Would her original title be more successful in directing the reader to the point of her novel than the one by which we all know it? To explore this, we will have to study how important first impressions really are in this novel and then consider if the social sins of pride and prejudice are what interested Jane Austen much more. Before we can do this, we will have to consider what

constituted pride in Jane Austen's view and the nature of the prejudice that arose from it.

You will see that the opening sentences are lively and challenging and these are followed by a statement on how the writer proposes to examine the question. He has also signalled that defining the terms 'pride' and 'prejudice' in this context will be left until later on. With the scope of the essay thus set out, the writer can go ahead with his discussion on the lines he has laid down for himself in his plan.

. . . And the ending

If all the arguments have been set out effectively in the body of the essay there should be no need to rehearse them all again in summary form at the end. The conclusion should be the final step in the argument to which the whole essay has been tending. Only if the essay has been long and closely argued might there be a case for reminding the reader of the main points before you state your conclusion. This may take the form of an adjudication between two or more opposing points of view which you have been discussing; it may be a last point which clinches all the previous arguments. Whatever its nature, it must give the impression of finality, that there is nothing more to be said. If possible, try to make the last sentence a direct response to the challenge of the title. For example, that essay question on the naming of Jane Austen's book might end: 'In view of all this, there can be no doubt that when Jane Austen changed her title to 'Pride and Prejudice' she did more than coin a memorable phrase: she pointed straight at the heart of her novel.'

Building a paragraph

'I can say all that there is to be said in half a page!' This is not the proud boast of a know-all but a cry of despair from a student who has worked out a good plan but cannot see how he is going to turn it into a thousand words or more. The techniques of paragraph building may vary from subject to subject, but common to most are variations on this pattern: link from the previous paragraph – key (or topic) sentence – expansion, explanation of the point or comment on it – illustration – supporting evidence – link towards the next paragraph.

This is not a scheme to be applied with mathematical precision to every paragraph. Providing that the key sentence is at the heart of the paragraph, all sorts of variations are possible. However, the scheme does show how a central idea can be developed and supported to make a paragraph of, say, a hundred words or more. This is not a matter of padding – something to be avoided at all times. It is the way to present each step in your discussion with adequate explanation and supporting evidence. No point should be made unless reasons for it can be given and evidence produced to substantiate it. Anyone assessing an essay will give little credit to arguments that are based on nothing more than a writer's assertion. A well-built paragraph should make the point, expand it and comment on it as necessary, illustrate it and set out the evidence on which it is based.

Here is a paragraph taken from the middle of an essay on 'Village Life in Late Twentieth-Century England'. (The village – and the statistics – are fictional! The numbers are inserted only to assist the commentary that follows.)

> (1) The influence of the Church may have changed considerably (2) but the decline in the role of the village shop has been even more noticeable. (3) As recently as twenty years ago, the village shop would have been the chief supplier of groceries and general provisions to the little community. Often it would have had a petrol pump and been a sub-post office. (4) In the village of Sidleigh in Mid-Devon, a survey revealed that 80% of a villager's shopping was done in the village shop. The neighbouring market town accounted for the other 20%. (5) Surveys also showed that this pattern of spending was typical of the county as a whole. (6) Now the situation is quite different and the reasons are not far to seek.

(1) is the link with the previous paragraph which had dealt with the Church.

(2) is the key sentence.

   (3) explains the position of the village shop before the decline set in.

   (4) gives an illustration from a named village.

   (5) adds supporting evidence from other surveys.

   (6) provides a link to the next paragraph which will explore the reasons for the decline.

The paragraph is 123 words long and the key idea has been stated, developed, explained, illustrated, supported by evidence and linked to the paragraphs before and after it.

Essay style

An academic essay is a piece of formal writing and its style must reflect this. Conversational expressions, slang, abbreviations (e.g. can't, won't, aren't) are out of place. Any essay is a kind of showpiece – it shows your teachers and examiners how much you know and how developed your thinking is – and therefore anything that gives an impression of casualness or lack of care must be avoided. You are expected to deploy all the qualities of clear English: well-made, grammatical sentences, correct spelling and careful paragraphing (which is evidence of good planning). If the essays are hand written, as most still are, they should be legible and attractively set out. It is a good idea to leave a line blank between each paragraph to lighten the appearance of the pages. Remember also to provide at least one wide margin per page for the teacher's comments. If you are quoting from a book, be sure to place the quotation between inverted commas; it is advisable to start on a new line for any quotation longer than a few words. Verse quotations should follow the line-by-line pattern of the original and not run on as if they were prose.

Summary

Make sure you fully understand the question.

If time permits, undertake any further reading and research you feel is needed.

Decide how you propose to treat the topic.

Use the brain-storming technique to list as many relevant ideas, etc. as you can.

From this material plan the paragraph headings of your essay before you begin to write.

Gain the interest of your reader by a good opening sentence.

Use the first paragraph to show how you interpret the question and how you propose to treat it. Define any terms if you think this is necessary.

Ensure that your argument develops clearly from paragraph to paragraph through the essay and reaches a satisfying conclusion.

Devise a last sentence that gives an impression of finality.

11 A Little Grammar

There are two common attitudes to grammar. One is shuddering horror at having to study anything so boring and useless; the other is a belief that if its complex rules can be mastered, then the ability to write superb English will be assured. Neither view is altogether reasonable. Grammar does not bore everyone and it is far from useless, but a mastering of all its rules will not guarantee your success as a writer. What is useful is a good understanding of how sentences are constructed and a familiarity with common grammatical terms so that we can discuss the language more easily. This is as much as will be attempted in this book and a great deal will be left out in order to keep the subject manageable.

Some useful terms

Noun

A word used for naming a person or thing, e.g. man, tree, mercy, London, group, fish, hope. What is called a proper noun refers to a particular person or place, e.g. John, Paris, Italy. A collective noun indicates a group, e.g. flock, audience, troop.

Pronoun

A word that takes the place of a noun, e.g. he, she, it, this, these, that, those.

Special kinds of pronouns include relative pronouns, e.g. who, whom, which, whose. These join clauses at the same time as standing for a noun, e.g. 'The girl found the key *which* I had lost.'

Adjective

A word that tells us more about a noun, e.g. red, old, delightful, angry, French, unjust, ten.

Verb

A word that says something about a person or thing. It can be thought of as a word indicating *doing* or *being*, e.g. the horses *ran*; truth *prevailed*; the cat *ate* the meat; the rain *is* falling; the holiday *will be* over soon.

Most forms of a verb can be used with a subject to make up a sentence. These forms are known as *finite verbs*. But three parts of a verb cannot be limited in this way and so are known as *infinitive verbs*. The three are the infinitive, the participle and the gerund.

The infinitive part of a verb names the action without referring to any person doing it and is usually introduced by 'to', e.g. to walk, to think, to have said, to have been.

Present participles (as in: he is *walking*) and past participles (he has *walked*) can be used as adjectives or verbs.

Examples of participles used as adjectives are: dancing girls; searching eyes; caring parent; a lost city; a scared child; the lighted lamp.

Examples of participles used verbally are: *running* too fast, he fell; the girls were *dancing*; her eyes had been *searching* his face; the parent was very *caring*; a child had been *scared*; the city was *lost* in the mist; the lamp will be *lighted*.

A gerund is a noun formed from a verb. It may look like a present participle but its function is different, since a participle can be used as an adjective whereas a gerund is a noun, e.g. *dancing* was permitted only on Thursdays; *stealing* is wrong; the visitors never enjoy *walking*; his hobby is *painting*.

Adverb

Although its name suggests that an adverb is a word which tells us more about a verb, it can also modify the meaning of any other word except a noun or a pronoun. In the following sequence, an adverb modifies in turn a verb, an adjective, another adverb, a preposition and a conjunction: the athlete ran *swiftly*; her face was *very* pale; he sang *quite* loudly; she walked *right* into the trap; we left *shortly* before the programme ended.

To put it another way, adverbs tell you how, why, when, where, on what condition and with what result, in connection with any part of speech except a noun or a pronoun!

Preposition

A word which stands before a noun or its equivalent to show its relationship to something else, e.g. the diver swam *under* the rocks; the lads wandered all *over* the town; we went *into* the house.

Conjunction

A word which joins sentences into one and also joins other words and phrases, e.g. and, but, either . . . or, if, since, because.

Talking about sentences . . .

There are a few technical terms that help us to talk about the way words are used within a sentence.

The *subject* of a sentence is the word (or words) about which something is said. The rest of the sentence, which says it, is called the *predicate*. In this sentence: 'The girl travelled to Scotland,' the word 'girl' is the subject and 'travelled to Scotland' is the predicate. You will notice that the predicate must always include a finite verb, otherwise nothing can be said!

In a sentence where the subject is doing something to another person or thing, the word referring to that recipient is called the *object*. In the following sentence: 'The workman hammered a nail,' the object is 'nail'. There can be no object following verbs such as 'to be' and 'to become'. The words that complete the sense of such a sentence are therefore called the *complement*. In this sentence: 'The travellers were tired and hungry,' the complement is 'tired and hungry'.

A *clause* is a sentence which has been made part of a larger one (see page 94).

A *phrase* is a group of two or more words which (unlike a clause) does not contain a subject and predicate.

What is a sentence?

The basic unit of expression is a sentence and you will not be secure in your writing – or punctuation – if you do not understand what a sentence is. Here is a definition as a starting point:

> A sentence is a group of words which express a complete thought. This means that something definite is said and for this to happen the group of words must contain a finite verb.

A few examples of short sentences and non-sentences will make this clear:

> Sentences: The cook baked the cake. The aircraft took off from Heathrow. Darkness covered the earth. The children played in the garden. The match had been lost.

(You will notice that in each sentence the statement is quite complete in itself and fully understandable on its own.)

> Non-sentences: when I saw him; jumping for joy; down the hill and around the town; if we ever get there; to see him eating.

(In contrast to a sentence, none of these groups of words makes complete sense – even though some of them contain verbs. They cannot be sentences, although all of them could of course be used as parts of sentences.)

Here are ten groups of words. Decide for yourself which are sentences and which are not. (The answers are given below.)

> (a) the lamp stood on the table; (b) in a blue gown trimmed with pearls; (c) which proved to be a grave mistake; (d) entering the hall and calling for the servants; (e) the countryside was particularly beautiful; (f) to find true happiness in this world; (g) people always enjoy seeing her on the stage; (h) because the work is too hard; (i) stealing a car and driving it away; (j) beside the house stood a small shed.

The sentences are (a), (e), (g), and (j). If you made a mistake, look at the group of words again and ask yourself if it is making complete sense as it stands. If so, it is a sentence.

All the examples of sentences given so far have been statements, but sentences can also take the form of questions or commands. The test is still: does the group of words make complete sense in itself?

> Questions: Will you come to see me today? Who is the strongest man on earth? Was Richard a good king or not?
> Commands: Bring me my dinner. Drive me home at once. Go!

Yes, even the single word 'Go!' is a sentence, because the message it conveys is complete in itself. (You will notice that 'Go!' is a verb and so fulfils the condition that every sentence must contain a finite verb.)

Kinds of sentence

The sentences we have been looking at so far by way of example have all been short and simple. In fact a sentence containing only one finite verb is known in grammar as a *simple sentence*. You will find that if you use a good number of simple sentences your writing will have directness and clarity. Your reader will be able to take in what you are saying quite easily because you are writing in short units. You yourself will also have benefited because you will have reduced the complications of what was in your mind to manageable proportions. Here, as an example of the use of simple sentences, is an extract from a letter dealing with arrangements for a charity fashion show:

> . . . The show will begin at eight o'clock. The models are arriving by taxi shortly after seven. They will need a large dressing room with at least two full-length mirrors. Mrs Granger, the owner of the boutique, will introduce the show herself. You and your friends have only to sell the tickets. The secretary of the hall committee will deal with all front-of-house problems. There is therefore very little you have to do . . .

By using only simple sentences, the writer has kept the information direct and to the point. This is very desirable and it would be hard to fault this letter if you judge it merely as a conveyer of certain facts. But does it entirely satisfy you as a piece of communication between two people who, we presume, are on friendly terms with each other? The writer has passed on efficiently the details of the arrangements for the fashion show, but what do you think of the tone of the letter? How would you react if you were the recipient? You might well think that this was a cold and unfriendly letter. The style is abrupt and the writer seems to be giving orders instead of seeking co-operation. By using only simple sentences, the writer has undoubtedly achieved clarity, but at the expense of any hint of graciousness. What is more, there is a jerkiness in the style and a lack of connection between each short sentence and the next.

Writing in simple sentences is an excellent discipline and should lead to great clarity in your expression. But such sentences are better used together with other kinds of sentences so that your style is flexible, varied and much more interesting than a long succession of simple sentences would be. This is particularly true if you are writing at length. A short business letter, making an appointment or requesting information, might well consist of just a few simple sentences; but an article, an essay or a long personal letter demands the variety and subtlety that longer and more complicated sentences can give. Let's look at ways of creating other kinds of sentences.

The easiest way to move beyond a string of short sentences is to join two or three of them together by conjunctions (e.g. 'and', 'but', 'or'). This creates what in grammar is called a compound sentence, for example:

> You will enjoy living in this house and your wife will love the garden.
> A holiday abroad is exciting but staying at home is cheaper.
> Either you do what I say or you leave my office at once.
> John will be home early tonight and so we can have supper at six.

You will notice that each example consists of two simple sentences which have been joined together by conjunctions. You can create quite long sentences with three or four little sentences within them.

A sentence which has become part of a longer one is called a *clause*. The following compound sentences each consists of four such clauses:

> He sold his car and bought a boat but he hated the sea and disliked the company of yachtsmen.
>
> The shopping precinct is lavishly decorated and has a remarkable range of shops, but it is overcrowded and lacks any sense of style.

As you see, the use of 'and' and 'but' helps you to build larger units and produce smoother writing than simple sentences on their own. The letter about the charity fashion show, used as an example above, would be improved if some of the simple sentences were combined into compound ones and the order slightly rearranged:

> . . . The show will begin at eight o'clock but the models are arriving by taxi shortly after seven. They will need a large dressing room with at least two full-length mirrors. Mrs Granger, the owner of the boutique, will introduce the show herself and the secretary of the hall committee will deal with all the front-of-house problems, and so you and your friends have only to sell the tickets. There is therefore very little that you have to do . . .

Already the tone of the letter has changed for the better and the flow of the passage has improved. All this has been achieved by joining together simple sentences with words that link them but do not alter their status within the new and bigger sentences.

Even more effective, however, is a technique which highlights only one of the sentences and places the others around it in a supporting role. The one chosen to carry the principal statement is called the *main clause* and those in a supporting role are called *subordinate clauses*. An example should make clear what happens. Here are three simple sentences:

> *Macbeth* is a very popular play. Booking has had to open early. Repairs to the theatre are not yet complete.

The writer decides to combine these and make the second sentence the main clause of the new sentence. The other two sentences will no longer be able to stand on their own but will depend on the main clause. In other words, they become its subordinate clauses. The new sentence is as follows:

> Because *Macbeth* is a very popular play, booking has had to open early, even though repairs to the theatre are not yet complete.

A sentence which contains one main clause and one or more subordinate clauses is known as a *complex sentence*. The ability to use such sentences with confidence is the mark of a skilled writer. There is nothing mysterious about them. We all use complex sentences in our conversation with great frequency:

> I bought this coat at a sale, although I'm not sure it fits me.
> If you don't like your dinner, you can go to a take-away.
> Before you say a word, look at this report.
> The man who lives next door has bought himself a Rolls.

You are of course very familiar with such sentences and use them all the time in ordinary speech, although you may not have known that grammarians call them *complex sentences*. This is like the character in a famous French comedy: when he was informed that prose was all language not written in verse-form, he declared with delight, 'Why, I've been speaking prose all my life!' Similarly, complex sentences are very often on our lips, even if we do not know what they are called. Understanding their grammatical structure, however, should give us more confidence to use them correctly and effectively when we write. It will also help considerably in knowing how to punctuate.

A complex sentence, you will remember, consists of one main clause and at least one subordinate clause – and there are three kinds of subordinate clauses:

Adjectival clauses

These are introduced by 'who', 'whom', 'which', 'whose', 'that' (i.e. relative pronouns). The job of such words is twofold: they join clauses together and, being pronouns, they stand in place of a noun or its equivalent. Here are two simple sentences:

The driver crashed his car. The driver was travelling too fast.

By making the second sentence subordinate to the first, we create the complex sentence:

The driver, who was travelling too fast, crashed his car.

The subordinate clause ('who was travelling too fast') is known as an adjectival clause because it is telling us more about the noun 'driver'.

The following list gives further examples of complex sentences containing adjectival subordinate clauses. You will notice that in each sentence there is only one main clause carrying the central piece of information. To this is joined at least one subordinate adjectival clause (printed in italic):

We met the girl *whose brother won the race.*
The village, *which lies in a valley*, is well protected.
The furniture *that we sold them* fetched five hundred pounds.
The child *to whom we gave the book* was obviously disappointed.
The student, *who had spent all his grant*, tried to borrow from his friend, *who was equally penniless herself.*

(Note: because adjectival clauses are introduced by relative pronouns they are also known as *relative clauses*. There is some special advice, to be found on page 108, on how to punctuate relative clauses.)

Adverbial clauses

These subordinate clauses usually modify the meaning of the verb in the main clause by referring to such things as time, place, manner, purpose, etc. related to it — hence the name adverbial. They are introduced by words such as 'if', 'although', 'because', 'since', 'before', 'after', 'when', 'while', etc. To be an efficient writer you do not need to be able to identify all the kinds of adverbial clauses, but we print their names in brackets after each example in case you are interested. Each subordinate clause is in italic:

They will come tomorrow *if we invite them.* (condition)
Although the weather is poor, we will set sail tonight. (contrast or concession)
The house will be built *before you can find the money for it.* (time)
Because she smiles easily, people like her. (reason)
He tried *so hard that he nearly died in the attempt.* (result)
If you behave like that, you deserve all you get. (condition)
They dug up the forest *so that they could plant crops.* (purpose)
The men slept *where they had dropped.* (place)

Noun clauses

These are groups of words containing a finite verb which do the work of a noun and can therefore take the place of one in the structure of a sentence. For example:

They forgot *that he was going away.*
What he thinks is quite unimportant.
That you consistently lied in this case will go against you in court.
We were unaware *that she had already gone.*
The information *that he had betrayed us* was a stunning blow.

Trying it out . . .

One way of avoiding a succession of simple sentences is by using complex sentences containing adjectival clauses. Try rewriting the following passage, replacing some of these simple sentences with complex ones. There is no need to remove every simple sentence – just enough to improve the flow and give variety to the passage:

The great house stood on the edge of town. It was surrounded by a high wall. Ugly pieces of glass had been fixed into it by the owner. The man was desperately scared of intruders. His gardeners were forbidden to work near the perimeter except to cut the grass. He supervised this operation himself. His butler had served him for thirty years. His principal duty was to deter visitors. A visitor would be bold to approach that front door.

Use simple, compound and complex sentences to improve the style of the following passage. You may of course alter the word order and make any other changes you think desirable:

The Saturday shoppers jostled their way through the market. They elbowed each other aside. They paid little attention to the crying babies and fractious children. The market constable was usually a fairly cheerful man. Today he looked strained and bewildered. A crowd such as this was unusual. It was not even Christmas. That he could have understood. At Christmas the whole town descended on the market at one time. At Christmas there were people at the gates even before opening time. Today, however, a long queue had formed before nine o'clock. The gates had opened at nine. At that time there had been some ugly scenes.

Variety

Do you notice anything about the sentence structures of the following short passage:

John Earlton stared across the frozen wastes of Antarctica. He had left base camp three days previously with only two companions. They were now sleeping in their tent. The men were thoroughly exhausted. John wondered about their chances of survival. The dogs were huddled in the snow beside the sledges. They too were feeling the strain.

The passage is clear enough and not badly written, but did you notice that each sentence followed a similar pattern? Each began with the subject of the sentence (John Earlton, He, They, The men, The dogs, They). This is not grammatically incorrect but it is very dull. Already the reader must be registering the mechanical quality of the writing and hoping for some variety in the sentence structure. This can be achieved by making each sentence begin in a different way. For example, you can begin with a subordinate clause, with a participle phrase, with a short non-verbal phrase, with an infinitive (e.g. *To see him drink* was a joy). With these ideas in mind, we can make the passage about the Antarctic explorers less rigid. The flexible structure will allow us to include more interesting details too:

> Shielding his eyes against the glare of the snow, John Earlton stared across the frozen wastes of Antarctica. He had left base camp three days previously with only two companions. Thoroughly exhausted by their ordeal, the men were sleeping in their tent while John wondered if they would survive their gruelling task. As for the dogs, they were huddled miserably in the snow. Even they were feeling the strain.

You will see that no sentence begins in the same way as the one before or after it.

If you are in the happy position of having plenty to write about and ideas are tumbling from your pen, then you are not expected to pause over each sentence and ponder its structure. You may well find that the excitement of writing is producing a lively style as you go along. But this will be the first draft. When you have finished it, you must read it over and edit it. This is the time to be aware of sentence structure and to check quite deliberately that there is variety in the way the sentences are built.

Be alert too to the *length* of your sentences. A succession of short sentences will soon become irritating, while a trail of very long ones will make the passage difficult to follow. Ensure that there is variety in the length of your sentences as well as in their structure.

Trying it out

Write half a dozen sentences about getting up in the morning and make each sentence begin in a different way from the others. Vary the length of the sentences too. Make an effort to include at least one simple, one compound and one complex sentence. As has already been said, you are unlikely to write in this artificial way when you are writing for yourself. This is an exercise to make you aware of the resources you have as a writer which you may be glad to call on when you are editing a first draft that seems more stilted than you thought it would be.

Summary

A sentence is a group of words that express a complete thought.

A simple sentence consists of only one main clause.

A compound sentence consists of two or more main clauses joined by conjunctions.

A complex sentence consists of a main clause and at least one subordinate clause.

There are three kinds of subordinate clauses—adjectival, adverbial and noun.

A lively style of writing can be achieved by using a variety of sentence structures.

12 Punctuation

The modern trend is to streamline punctuation, doing away with unnecessary commas (for example, in the heading of letters) and pages spattered with dots and dashes. Today the colon is rarely used except to introduce an explanation or a list of items and the semicolon is already under threat. Is this a matter for regret or congratulation? Certainly a great deal of old-fashioned punctuation served no useful purpose, for the meaning was perfectly plain without it. On the other hand, clear English is much enhanced if the writer can assist the reader by showing how he wishes words to be phrased. Some people still decide their punctuation according to the length of pause they think they would like between word groups – a comma for a short pause, a semicolon for a longer one and a full stop for a very long pause. This method may be helpful to very young children but it is a most unreliable guide for older people. Punctuation is, for the most part, based on grammar. Learning just a few grammatical principles will give you the confidence to punctuate effectively.

Full stop

This most important piece of punctuation is used to mark the end of a sentence. In the section on grammar, the sentence was defined as *a group of words which expresses a complete thought.* Here is such a sentence: 'The owner sold his business.' There would be little or no difficulty in identifying that as a sentence and placing a full stop at the end of it. Problems arise when the sentence grows longer by additions before and after that main statement:

> Since times were difficult the owner sold the business to his brother he quickly disposed of it to a relative who had more money than sense it was not a wise purchase

Where should we put the full stops in this short passage? To put that question another way, how many sentences are there? The answer is three since there are three groups of words expressing complete thoughts. At the heart of our first sentence is the original statement 'the owner sold the business', which has been extended by 'Since times were difficult' at the beginning and 'to his brother' at the end. Note that neither of these additional groups are complete statements in themselves and therefore they cannot be sentences. They can only be part of the sentence about the owner selling his business. The first full stop must therefore come after 'brother'.

A common error would be to place a comma, rather than a full stop, after 'brother' because the writer wrongly felt that as 'brother' and 'he' were identical in meaning they should not be so firmly separated. This is false and ungrammatical thinking. A full stop is needed because one complete statement has finished and another is about to begin.

The heart of the second sentence is 'He quickly disposed of it' and this is extended by 'to a relative who had more money than sense' — words which cannot stand on their own as a sentence because they are incomplete without the first group.

Many people would now wish to put a comma after 'sense'. Wrong again. Their argument that 'it' looks an unimportant little word is unacceptable. The only test is the grammatical one: is the group of words 'it was not a wise purchase' expressing a complete thought or not? Obviously the answer is that it does express a complete thought and so it is a sentence and must be placed between full stops. Correctly punctuated, the sentences would be:

> Since times were difficult, the owner sold the business to his brother. He quickly disposed of it to a relative who had more money than sense. It was not a wise purchase.

Sometimes people are reluctant to put a full stop because the sentence under consideration is very short: 'the sun shone the sky was blue.' A full stop should be placed after 'shone' and not a comma, even though the word groups are short and closely connected in meaning. If you are dissatisfied with 'The sun shone. The sky was blue.' you should reconsider your phrasing and not the rules of punctuation. The word 'and' would join these two short sentences into one and produce a better effect: 'The sun shone and the sky was blue.' Later on we will see how a semicolon can be of use in joining two short sentences.

The only time you may use commas at the end of sentences is when there are several forming a sequence, with a conjunction linking the last two (in effect, producing a single, complex sentence): e.g. 'The sun shone, the sky was blue, the water sparkled and our boat lay ready for sea.'

Full stops are also used when a word is abbreviated (Oct. Capt. Rev.) although a full stop is not added when the abbreviation ends with the same letter as the complete word (Dr Mr Mrs).

Question mark

A question mark (?) must be placed at the end of every direct question. For example:

> Where are you going? Did they see the film? How deep is the river? Will you come to our office or shall we meet in town?

Note that the question mark incorporates a full stop and therefore must be placed at the end of the sentence. Note too that a question which is reported (and is therefore an *indirect* question) does not have a question mark. For example:

> 'Are you going to France?' (direct question);
> The travel agent asked if the man was going to France. (indirect question)

Exclamation mark

As its name implies, this mark follows an exclamation. Like the question mark, the exclamation mark incorporates a full stop and must be placed at the end of the sentence, for example:

> What a beautiful morning! How lonely she looks! What dreadful news! How brave of him!

Sometimes an exclamation is, strictly speaking, a question and will therefore be followed by a question mark:

> How could he bring himself to do it? What are we to think of her?

An exclamation mark can follow a single word or sound:

> Oh! Shame! Ha! No! Listen!

It is also used to draw attention to the unexpected or to make something sound dramatic:

> I opened the door and there she was! He dared to tell me he loved her!

Capital letters

A sentence must begin with a capital letter. Direct speech, quoted within a sentence, begins with a capital letter. The word 'I' is always written as a capital.

The particular names of persons and places (proper nouns) begin with capitals (e.g. John, Mary, Mr Thomas, Paris, Germany, Australia, January, Tuesday, River Seine, Mount Everest). Adjectives formed from proper nouns begin with a capital too (e.g. Italian, Napoleonic, Parisian, Mozartian).

Titles of books, plays, poems, newspapers and journals, musical works, ships, hotels, etc. use capitals. The first word and the last word always have a capital and so do all the other words except very small words such as 'the', 'a', 'and', 'of', 'if', etc. (e.g. *Death of a Salesman, News of the World, The Marriage of Figaro, Queen of the Pacific, To Kill a Mockingbird, She Stoops to Conquer*).

Comma

Two things may be said at once about commas: do not use them instead of full stops; only use them when they are really necessary or useful.

A comma marks a very short pause in the flow of a sentence and therefore is often used at the writer's discretion. Consider the slight difference that the comma makes in the second example:

> I walked into the room and there was a policeman.
> I walked into the room, and there was a policeman.

Although writers have this discretion, there are some occasions when commas are essential:

1 to separate items in a list. A comma is placed between each item except the last two, which are separated by 'and'. There is no comma after the last item.

> e.g. The builders had brought ladders, scaffolding, planks and pulleys in preparation for their work.

A similar rule applies to a succession of adjectives and other parts of speech as in:

> The dark, mysterious and silent forest.

However, commas between adjectives are used only when they can be interchanged without a feeling of awkwardness. The above example might have been phrased:

> The mysterious, silent and dark forest.

On the other hand, one would not wish to change the order of the adjectives in the following:

> The jolly young fellow had us all laughing.
> A lively little dog bounded up to us.

Commas would therefore not be used.

Sometimes the list will consist of phrases or clauses. Commas are used to separate them:

> Running the office, maintaining her home, looking after her elderly parents and helping her married daughter all took their toll.

2 around words in apposition. (A word or phrase placed beside another to give a fuller explanation is said to be in apposition to it.)

e.g. The President of the United States, Mr George Bush, was welcomed at the airport.

or: Mr George Bush, the President of the United States, was welcomed at the airport.

The Building Society manager, Mrs Lucy Jones, gave us a talk on her career.

3 around names and titles when used to address people:

Mary, I want you to listen carefully.
We think, George, that you must try once more.
The inspector is here to see you, sir.

4 around non-essential phrases:

By the way, have you met before?
The house, so they say, is haunted.
The project, I am afraid, must be cancelled.
The real reason is very different, I believe.

5 around words linking an argument, such as 'however', 'moreover', 'furthermore', 'on the other hand', 'nevertheless', etc:

The committee, however, decided against him.
I urge you, nevertheless, to be sympathetic to his problems.
The argument, moreover, was badly presented.

6 to mark off subordinate adverbial phrases and clauses where it will assist the reader. This is more likely to be at the beginning or in the middle of sentences than at the end:

If only you had told me, I would have telephoned her.
The doctor, although he was extremely busy, found time to visit my father.
Racing for the ball, the two players crashed into each other.
but: The secretary locked her desk because she was going out to lunch.

7 to mark off adjectival clauses if the subject matter is not an essential addition to the meaning (i.e. if the adjectival clause could be left out altogether without altering the meaning of the sentence):

> The actress, who was old and fat, still attracted large audiences.
>
> The house, which had been on the market for months, was sold to a retired couple from Manchester.
>
> The parking attendant, to whom we always give a tip, was not on duty last night.

NOTE: If the adjectival clause in some way modifies the meaning of the word it refers to, then *no commas are used.*

> e.g. The soldiers who were unshaven on parade must report to the sergeant-major.
>
> The manager wants to see all the assistants to whom he sent a warning letter.
>
> The tenants whose rents are overdue will face eviction.

In each of the above examples the meaning of the sentence would be changed if the adjectival clause was omitted. For instance, the sergeant-major does not want to see all the soldiers, but only those who were unshaven; the manager only wants to see the assistants to whom he has sent a letter, and the only tenants to face eviction are those whose rents are overdue. These adjectival clauses define 'soldiers', 'manager' and 'tenants' and so are essential to the meaning of the sentences. They are not, therefore, marked off by commas.

You will have noticed that two commas often act as a form of bracketing. It is therefore worth asking yourself when you put one comma if you should not be putting a second also, unless the bracketing is completed by the full stop at the end of the sentence, or if the comma comes after the first word or group in a sentence, since there cannot be a comma at the beginning of a sentence. The following sentences are incorrectly punctuated because the writer has inserted only one comma when two are needed. Decide for yourself where the missing commas should go:

Our London visitors, Mr and Mrs Crowden stayed for two
weeks.
The duty officer John White, was quickly on the scene.
We decided, before we knew anything about him that he
would be our choice.

Semicolon

The correct use of the semicolon is less well known than
that of the full stop and the comma and it is possible to survive
without it. On the other hand, the rules for its use are not difficult
to understand and it is a useful addition to a writer's resources.
Consider these two sentences:

The men gazed down the cliff. They knew the descent
would be dangerous.

The punctuation is perfectly correct but you may prefer your reader
to think of these statements as part of the same sentence. The effect
of bringing them together would be less abrupt than leaving them as
two separate sentences. Resist the temptation to insert a comma. Use
a semicolon:

The men gazed down the cliff; they knew the descent
would be dangerous.

There is no joining word (such as 'and') between the sentences. If
there were, a semicolon would be incorrect.

The rule is that a semicolon is used to bring together two sentences
(very often short ones) which are closely connected in meaning but
which are not linked by a conjunction (i.e. 'and' or 'but'). If the
subjects of the sentences are the same, as in the above example, the
semicolon is particularly appropriate. Here are some examples of its
use. In the first two, the subjects of two original sentences are the
same; in the other two they are different, but the meanings are closely
connected:

The cleaner moved into the office; she looked at her task
with distaste.

The secretaries sorted the pile of mail; they felt quite unable to cope with it all.

The students filed into the lecture room; the porter handed each a folder of notes.

Construction work was ahead of schedule; the engineer had been too cautious over his timing.

Note that the word after the semicolon begins with a small letter and not a capital.

The semicolon has another use. You will recall that items in a list – whether words or short phrases – are usually separated by commas. If, however, the items consist of longer word groups, then they are more effectively separated by semicolons. This is especially useful if the long word groups already contain commas, for the semicolons avoid any confusion that might otherwise arise.

e.g. Among the properties he acquired during his long career were a London theatre, complete with all its nineteenth-century furnishings; a stately home, which had never before been on the market; a block of flats at a seaside resort and a complete shopping mall in a city centre.

There is no semicolon between the last two items in the list, which are joined by 'and'.

Colon

The most common use of the colon is to introduce a list of items which explain or exemplify:

You must bring all these articles with you: towels, sheets, blankets, knife, fork and two spoons.

The best route to take is this: go down the hill to the station; turn left at the bottom; go to the first traffic lights; turn right and then bear left at the next fork. You will see our office on the right.

(Notice the use of semicolons between the items in the list of instructions.)

After the phrase 'as follows', most people would quite correctly place a colon. The habit of adding a dash to this (:–) is frowned on as being unnecessary. Limit yourself to the colon.

A colon is also used to separate a summarizing clause from other clauses in the sentence which explain or expand it:

> Heavy traffic created problems for those who lived in this part of the road: lorries frequently mounted the pavement to pass each other; diesel fumes filled the living-rooms and the noise of the vehicles was unbearable.

> Conference rooms with the most modern facilities; all bedrooms equipped with telephones, radios and colour TVs; three restaurants to cater for every taste and covered parking for three hundred cars: the Royal would be the best hotel in the city.

Dash

The dash is such a useful piece of punctuation that it should be used sparingly. There have been writers who have scattered dashes all over their pages, using them as substitutes for commas, semicolons and colons. This can lead to careless writing with random ideas inserted with little thought, aided and abetted by the ever-helpful dash. It is better to know what a dash can do and use it with understanding and discretion:

a) to emphasize a word or phrase for special effect:

> She opened her eyes and looked at his portrait – for the last time.

b) in pairs, to serve as brackets to mark off material additional to the sentence:

> He entered the council chamber – and his visit was totally unexpected – to announce to the senators that he had taken control.

c) to add a remark to the end of a sentence:

> The sky was very clear and the atmosphere strangely calm
> – never a good sign at this time of year.

d) to introduce material to amplify or explain what has been said (a use similar to that of a colon):

> The people must be prepared to make greater sacrifices –
> their homes, their possessions, their land and even their
> children.

Brackets

As we have seen when discussing commas and dashes, writers sometimes insert words or phrases into their sentences which are in some way additional to the main statement. These insertions are known as parentheses. There are three ways of setting them apart from the run of the sentence – by using commas, dashes or brackets. Which to choose is the writer's decision. A pair of commas is quite light punctuation; two dashes seem firmer and a pair of brackets shows very definitely that the material is an addition to the sentence. We already know that a pair of commas would be appropriate around such minor insertions as 'by the way', 'so they say', 'I am afraid', 'I believe', etc. For other additions the writer must use his or her judgement, remembering that brackets are useful for an explanatory word as well as for longer phrases or even complete sentences. The examples below show how brackets might be used, although in the second and third sentence another writer might have decided to use a pair of dashes:

> We found a restaurant specializing in crêpes (pancakes).
> His office was very smart (it had recently been renovated)
> and he was obviously proud of it.
> The party of visiting scientists (they were the chairman's
> special guests) were treated like royalty.

Hyphen

This should not be confused with the dash. A hyphen is a small horizontal stroke used to join words to make compounds or to attach prefixes to words when they would be ambiguous or awkward without it. In this way we can distinguish between 're-creation' and 'recreation', and easily understand 're-elect' instead of puzzling over 'reelect'. Hard and fast rules for the use of hyphens do not exist, but the following advice is offered for guidance:

a) place a hyphen between two adjectives if one or the other on its own would not make sense: e.g., a bold-faced man. (It is possible to say 'a bold man' but hardly a 'faced man'. Therefore 'bold-faced' needs a hyphen.)

b) use a hyphen where its absence would make the meaning uncertain: e.g., a small-coal merchant. (This shows that the merchant is selling small coal, whereas if the hyphen had been omitted it might appear that the coal merchant himself was small!)

c) use a hyphen where a prefix cannot conveniently become part of the word without it: e.g., semi-conscious, counter-intelligence, multi-faceted, re-lay (to distinguish the word from 'relay').

Apostrophe

There are two common uses for the apostrophe ('): one is to indicate possession and the other is to show the omission of one or more letters in a word.

To show possession

Add an s to the word and place an apostrophe *before* the s if the possessor is singular, and *after* the s if there are two or more possessors.

> e.g. the soldier's helmet, the farmer's tractors, the tree's branches, the cliff's edge, love's gift, the road's surface.

The apostrophe placed *before* the s in these examples shows that we are speaking of only one soldier, one farmer, one tree, one cliff, one love and one road.

If we place the apostrophe *after* the s, we are immediately signalling to the reader that in each example we are talking about two or more possessors. For example, 'the soldiers' helmet' suggests that two or more soldiers are sharing one helmet; 'the farmers' tractors' must refer to two or more farmers owning the tractors; 'the trees' branches' refer to the branches on a number of trees, and so on.

Exceptions Three of the most common plural words in the English language (and one less common these days) have the apostrophe *before* the s to indicate possession: 'men', 'women', 'children', 'brethren':

> e.g., 'the men's room', 'the women's clothes', 'the children's toys', 'the brethren's decision'.

If the placing of the apostrophe continues to confuse you, think of it as a little arrow pointing back at the possessor(s). This would be particularly helpful with the exceptions just mentioned. You will notice that the apostrophes are pointing back quite correctly to the words 'men', 'women', 'children', 'brethren', since you are conveying 'the room of the men', 'the clothes of the women', 'the toys of the children', 'the decision of the brethren'. Similarly, it points back to 'farmer' (the farmer's tractors) or farmers (the farmers' tractors).

A little problem arises with names ending in s (e.g. Jones, Phillips, Harkness, Rees, Gladys). This can be solved by adding an extra s and placing the apostrophe before it:

> Mr Jones's house, Mrs Phillips's shop, John Harkness's pony, Megan Rees's recipes, Gladys's birthday.

It is permissible to leave out the additional s and put the apostrophe at the end of the name itself and this is often done in longer names: e.g. Mrs Phillips' shop.

It is the custom never to add an extra s to a classical name. We would therefore write: Socrates' philosophy, Demosthenes' speech, Brutus' plot.

Apostrophes in abbreviations

An apostrophe shows the omission of one or more letters in an abbreviation: aren't (are not), didn't (did not), couldn't (could not), haven't (have not).

Note the special cases: shan't (shall not), can't (cannot), won't (will not).

A notorious trap is the abbreviation 'it's' (it is). Without the apostrophe, the word becomes 'its', a possessive pronoun (like 'his' or 'hers'). The distinction is illustrated by the following sentences:

> *It's* hard to believe that the house lost *its* roof in the fire.
> My dog sits in *its* kennel when *it's* raining.

Do not use an apostrophe with abbreviations which have become words through accepted usage. It is no longer necessary to write: 'phone, 'plane, 'bus. Nor are apostrophes needed with the *s* in contractions such as 'MPs' or 'QCs', nor after dates such as 'the 1990s'. They are only necessary to avoid confusion, as with single letters: e.g. There are two i's in the name 'Miriam'.

Punctuating dialogue

1 Inverted commas (also known as quotation marks) – either single or double – are placed around the actual words of the speaker.

2 The words spoken are separated from the rest of the sentence by a comma. If the sentence ends with the quotation, only one full stop is needed and this is placed inside the inverted commas. If the sentence continues beyond the quotation, a comma is placed within the inverted commas and the final full stop is reserved for the end of the sentence.

3 The first word spoken in each quotation begins with a capital letter unless it is the continuation of a quoted sentence which has already begun.

4 A new paragraph is required with every change of speaker. For example:

> The child said, 'My legs are tired.'

'That's because you never rest them,' her mother replied with a smile.

'But I rest them at night,' answered the child, 'when I'm in bed. I can never sit still during the day.'

Her mother had no answer to that.

You will notice that the words of both the mother and the child are within inverted commas and that the comma after 'rest them' and 'at night' in the second and third sentences are inside the inverted commas. Note too that in the third sentence a comma is needed after the author's insertion 'answered the child'. All the quotations begin with a capital letter, except for the words 'when I'm in bed' since this is merely a continuation of a sentence. The passage also shows that a new paragraph begins with every change of speaker and when the author continues the story. You will notice that the child's last remark consists of two uninterrupted sentences and the inverted commas do not close the quotation until she has finished both of them.

If the quoted remarks take the form of a question or exclamation, they will of course end with a question mark or an exclamation mark:

'How did you find your way here?' he asked.

She avoided his question and swept her eyes around the untidy room, cluttered with paint pots and unwashed dishes.

She looked at him with distaste and exclaimed, 'What a dreadful place to live!'

Notice that the question mark and the exclamation mark are inside the inverted commas and that the question mark takes over the place where there would otherwise be a comma.

Single or double . . .? There is no hard and fast rule about using single or double inverted commas in dialogue, except to make your choice and stick to it. In the examples given above, single inverted commas have been used but they could be replaced by double ones: "How did you find your way here?" he asked.

You sometimes have to quote a title or another remark within someone's speech. For this purpose you use the kind of inverted commas (single or double) not in use as the main speech marks:

> 'When you said, "I'll give you a thousand pounds," did you really mean it?' I asked incredulously.

Other uses of inverted commas

In addition to their important use in punctuating dialogue, inverted commas single or double, indicate:

a) titles of books, plays, music, etc. as in: Last week I saw 'The Merry Wives of Windsor' and tomorrow I am going to the opera to hear Verdi's 'Falstaff'.

Note, however, that in printed material (as against written or typed material) titles of books, plays, music, etc. are printed in *italics*.

b) Words and phrases mentioned for discussion or special consideration; e.g. Some people are offended by the modern use of 'hopefully' instead of 'I hope that'.

c) The names of ships, cars, trains etc. as in: The old man remembered sailing on the 'Mauretania' and the 'Queen Mary', but regretted that he had never travelled on the 'Flying Scotsman'.

Again, note that in printed material, these names are printed in *italics*.

d) Quotations from other pieces of writing, for example:

> Whenever I see a rainbow, I always think of Wordsworth's lines,
> 'My heart leaps up when I behold
> A rainbow in the sky.'

13 *Spelling*

If only we could reduce English spelling to a few simple rules! Unfortunately the rich and complex history of English words has produced spellings which smother most rules with exceptions while the rules themselves can be so difficult to understand and apply that it is often easier to learn a word parrot-fashion or look it up in a dictionary. Help for poor spellers has already arrived with pocket computers that offer you the spelling you are looking for at the touch of a few buttons, and word processors which check your text, point out your spelling errors and suggest corrections. Such assistance will be welcomed by the army of poor spellers, but they all have one disadvantage – they are time consuming. Just to look up a word in a dictionary can take as much as a minute or more. (Try using the index of a Thesaurus, which gives all the words uncluttered by definitions and derivations.) If you want to write fluently and with confidence the ability to spell words in common use is essential.

One obstacle to helping the poor speller is that the reason for his or her weakness may be quite obscure. At the far end of the spectrum is the dyslexic, who suffers from an abnormality of word perception which makes learning to read and spell a matter for specialist teaching. But many people who are not dyslexic and whose problems are less severe nevertheless find difficulty in recognizing and remembering letter sequences and word shapes for reasons that may never be apparent to them or their teachers. Others find they can master the spelling of difficult words with very little effort. If you do have a spelling problem, there seems to be no easy answer at present except the old advice: identify the words that cause you trouble; look up the correct spellings; write them down and memorize them.

The *eye* is the most important organ in learning to spell: look at the shape of the word; observe where double letters occur; identify the part of the word you usually get wrong and look carefully at what is correct. Write down the correct version a number of times, *thinking about what you are doing* and then look closely at what you have done.

Despite the fact that English pronunciation is notorious for being

a very unreliable guide to English spelling, the *ear* does have a part
to play. Careless pronunciations may lead to misspellings. If you say
'I'm reely intrested in our libry', you may find yourself spelling the
words in that way instead of correctly: 'I'm really interested in our
library'. Make sure that it is not the mis-pronunciation of a troublesome word that is leading you astray. (This happened to the student
who named the longest river in the USA *Mrs Sippi!*)

Learning words in groups is a great help since the knowledge of
one spelling will recall that of a similar word. Some useful groupings
are given below. Rules of course have their place and will sometimes
provide the answer to a spelling problem, though one has to be
aware that there are many exceptions. Numerous rules are hard to
remember and half learned rules are dangerous: most people can
chant, '*i* before *e* except after *c*', even if they do not always apply it.
But this rule is inaccurate unless you add '. . . when the sound is
ee'. We will therefore limit ourselves to six rules which you may
find helpful, beginning with the famous one just mentioned.

Spelling rules

1 *i* comes before *e* except after *c* when the sound is *ee*
(as in *speed*):

> without *c*: believe, field, brief, achieve, grief.
> with *c*: receive, receipt, conceive, ceiling, deceive.
> *exceptions*: seize, weir, weird.

2 Do not change the spelling of a word when adding a prefix to it
or when adding a suffix that begins with a consonant.

*A prefix is a group of letters added to the beginning of a word (e.g.
dis- un- in- ad-). A suffix is a group of letters added to the end of a
word (e.g. -ment -ness -ing -ly)*:

> adding prefixes: necessary–unnecessary, spelling–mis-
> spelling, satisfy–dissatisfy, ride–override.
> adding suffixes: keen–keenness, sincere–sincerely, en-
> courage–encouragement, beautiful–beautifully.
> *exceptions*: argue–argument, true–truly.

In a few words, the final -e is retained before -ing and -er to distinguish them from similar words:

> singe–singeing (sing–singing), dye–dyeing (die–dying).

The final -e is also retained after a c or g in order to keep the sound of the consonant 'soft', as in:

> change–changeable, manage–manageable, notice–noticeable, peace–peaceable.

3 Doubling the consonant after a stressed long vowel makes the vowel sound short:
(Note: the vowel sounds, a e i o u, are long when they are pronounced as in aid, seen, ride, nose, rude. They are short as in sat, fed, lip, toss, rut.)

> long vowel: doping, taping, later, piped, bony, hoping.
> short vowel: dropping, tapping, latter, pipped, bonny, hopping.

4 Drop one *l* from a word ending *ll* when you combine it with another to make a new word.

> plenty + full – plentiful; well + come – welcome; full + fill – fulfil (note how each word loses an l); all + together – altogether.
> *exceptions*: unfortunately there are several exceptions to this rule, including hillside, footfall, illness, etc.

5 When you add to words ending in y, change the y to an i if the letter before the y is a consonant:

> lady–ladies, cherry–cherries, fancy–fancies, merry–merriment.

If the letter before the y is a vowel, do not change the y:

> toy–toys, monkey–monkeys, array–arraying, buy–buying, grey–greying.

6 Most words ending in -*o* become plural by adding an *s*, but a few add -*es*:

> photos, embryos, radios, studios, folios
> but heroes, potatoes, tomatoes, cargoes.

These six rules should not be too difficult to understand, remember and apply. Beyond them, however, such rules as there are become of limited value and exceptions abound – as they do, alas, even to the six rules above. It is better now to identify your own weaknesses and find out what is, for you, the best way of learning to correct them. A well-tried method is to learn similar words in groups. Observe what they have in common and learn them together.

A learning hint: record the groups on a personal cassette recorder, speaking at dictation speed. As you play them back, write them down. Use the pause button if you need a longer time to think. Then check your spellings from the printed list. Set yourself a learning plan, such as so many groups per day or per week. You could also make up sentences containing as many of the difficult words as possible, record them and play them back to yourself while you take them down as dictation. Two such passages are included at the end of this chapter. The words are taken from the word groups and from the list of 150 words often misspelled printed on pages 124–5.

Word groups

In each group you will find some words you can spell with ease alongside others which cause problems. Choose a familiar word as the key to each group and link the other words to this key word in your mind. Look for the common factor within each group. For example, the first group is made up of words beginning *acqua-*; the usual error is to leave out the *c*.

> acquaint, acquire, acquit(ted), acquiesce;
> advice (noun) – advise (verb), practice (noun) – practise (verb), licence (noun) – license (verb);

apparent, correspondent, excellent, existence, experience, independent, negligent, prominent;

business, cosiness, easiness;

chief, belief, thief, grief;

chord, chorus, choreography, choir;

committee, committed, accommodation;

conscious, conscience, conscientious;

doctor, professor, councillor, counsellor, governor, surveyor;

feather, heather, weather (rain & sunshine);

forecast, forefather, foremost, foresee, foretell, forebode, forestall;

here, there, where, whereas, whether (or not);

illegible, illegal, illegitimate, illiterate, illicit, illogical, illuminate, illusion, illustrious;

indeed, exceed, proceed, succeed;

but accede, precede, recede, intercede, supersede, concede;

pair, despair, repair, impair;

playwright, shipwright, wheelwright;

rhythm, rhyme, rheumatic, rhapsody, rhinoceros, rhubarb;

superintend, supercilious, supersede, supervise.

One or two words?

There are often errors (even in books and newspapers) over the division of some much-used words and phrases. These are the correct versions:

all right (not alright), a lot of (not alot of), into, on to, whereas, in fact.

Distinguish between: already (He has already arrived) and all ready (We are all ready to leave); altogether (Altogether, it was a most enjoyable evening) and all together (The family enjoyed being all together).

Trying it out

Here are some passages containing many common spelling problems. Record them on tape so that you can play them back to yourself and write them down. Speak fairly slowly and use the pause button as necessary. You can repeat these dictations a number of times until you are able to write them perfectly. You could make up further passages for yourself incorporating the words that cause you special problems. You may be able to persuade a friend to read the passages to you at dictation speed – but a tape recorder is likely to be more long-suffering!

1 There was chaos in my family when I read out the advertisement for a holiday in the Mediterranean. The excitement was so intense that I did not succeed in making myself heard for a full five minutes. Then my husband wanted to know more about the accommodation, being very suspicious of foreign hotels. I saw the holiday as an opportunity to gain independence from the kitchen and was desperately anxious that we should not go camping. I could guarantee from bitter experience that I would be the one who had to queue at the camp supermarket and have the privilege of doing all the cooking. For my two daughters the holiday was inevitably the occasion for endless arguments about the clothes and jewellery they should take. We all realized that to Jane a holiday meant a marvellous excuse to acquire an extraordinary amount of new clothes, whereas Elizabeth preferred to embarrass us all by wearing the weirdest garments she could discover. When at last they were quiet enough for us to discuss things reasonably, it quickly became apparent that the only intelligent decision would be for us all to have separate holidays, since it was noticeable that each of us was too independent to acquiesce in anyone else's scheme!

2 Quite definitely neighbours can be a nuisance! Undoubtedly many can be friendly and endeavour to be

agreeable, discussing the weather or their rheumatism when you meet them in the street or over the garden wall. But occasionally you encounter one who is at best a nuisance and at worst a menace. I once lived next door to a colleague from the bank where I worked as a secretary. He was one of those excessively efficient people who are so conscientious that he could not conceive of anyone wanting to forget the bank after five o'clock. As I was so accessible at home, he was always knocking on my door to show me correspondence and reports of committees that he had brought home, no doubt illegally. He sincerely believed that I would be delighted to discuss business matters in the evenings until I told him bluntly that I preferred television in my leisure time to unnecessary and irrelevant conversation that benefited neither of us.

One hundred and fifty words often misspelled

Accessible, accidentally, accommodation, acquaintance, acquiesce, acquire, acquit(ted), address, advertisement, agreeable, already, amount, apparent, arctic, argument;
basically, beautiful, beginning, believe, benefit(ed), business;
chaos, colleague, committee, comparative, comparison, conceive, conscientious, correspondence, council (an assembly), counsel (advice);
definite, description, desperately, developed, difference, discipline;
efficient, eighth, embarrass, endeavour, environment, exaggerate, exceed, excessive, excitement, existence, experience, extraordinary;
family, favourite, foreign, foresee, fulfil(led);
gauge, government, grammar, grievous, guarantee, guard;
handkerchief, harass, height, heir, hero(es), humour;
illegible, illiterate, immediately, impair, independence, instalment, intelligent, interested, irrelevant;
jealous, jewellery;
knowledge;
leisure, loose, lose;

maintenance, marvellous, meant, Mediterranean, miniature, miscellaneous, mischievous, monastery;

necessary, negligent, neighbour, noticeable, nuisance;

occasion (occurred, occurrence), offer(ed), opportunity;

parallel(ed), parliament, picnic(ked), playwright, precede, prefer(red), prejudice, privilege, procedure, proceed;

quarter, queue, quiet, quite;

receive, refer(red), referee, reign, resistance, rheumatism, rhythm;

secretary, seize, separate, sincerely, skilful, summarize, superintend, supersede, surprise;

temporary, tendency, tie (tying), tragedy, truly, twelfth;

undoubtedly, unnecessary, until;

valuable, veterinary, vicious,

weather, weir, weird, whereas, whether, wilful, worship(ped);

yacht, yield, yoke (of oxen), yolk (of an egg).

14 Words

They sound similar

The path to clear English is strewn with a number of traps well known to experienced travellers across this field, but likely to ensnare the inexperienced or unwary. Some of these occur when one word sounds exactly like another but is spelled differently and carries a different meaning (e.g. 'hoard' and 'horde'); others are pronounced and spelled differently but are easy to confuse (e.g. *flout* and *flaunt*). Below there is a list of some of these pitfalls:

Affect – effect

Although the pronunciation of these two words is similar, they are quite distinct in meaning.

Affect is commonly used only as a verb and it means 'to act as an influence on someone or something'. In a way, it *alter*s a situation and you might find it useful to remember that the first letter of *alter* and *affect* is the same. For example:

> Your unpunctuality will affect your progress in the firm.
> Their decision affected the business at once.
> His bad driving seriously affected my confidence in him.

Effect is a verb but it can also be a noun. As a verb, it means 'to bring about or accomplish something', as in:

> The new manager is going to effect several changes in our routine.
> The garage mechanic quickly effected the repairs to my car.
> The doctor effected a remarkable cure.

As a noun, *effect* means the result or consequence of an action:

> The effect of his policy was disastrous.
> Changing the wallpaper had the effect of making the room seem smaller.

Alternate – alternative

Alternate, as an adjective, means 'every other one' or 'changing by turns'. For example:

>You may park on this side of the road on alternate days.
>Alternate pages are left blank for your notes.

As a verb, it means to change in the manner indicated above:

>Parking alternates from day to day in this road.
>My duties alternate with my friend's.

An *alternative* is a choice between two or more things. Strictly speaking, it should only be used when there are two choices, but it is now commonly accepted that there can be several choices. For example:

>I had no alternative but to accept his offer.
>As the family could not afford a holiday abroad, the only alternative was a visit to Torquay.

Appraise – apprise

Appraise means 'to assess the value or quality', for example:

>The farmer rapidly appraised the worth of the animal.
>She appraised the job applicant from his CV.

Apprise means 'to inform or notify'. It has an old-fashioned ring to it:

>I will apprise you of my decision when I have studied your report.
>We were not apprised of the bank's intentions before yesterday.

Aural – oral

The education world makes frequent use of these two words as they are to do with listening and speaking. Unfortunately, they are not always distinguished in people's minds. *Aural* is to do with hearing and *oral* with speaking. Their Latin origins make this plain: 'aural' comes from *auris* (Latin for ear) and 'oral' comes from *os* (Latin for mouth). Thus it would be correct to refer to a listening test as an aural test (say, in music or a foreign language). An examination which involves speaking aloud would be an 'oral'. Both words have the same pronunciation, which does not help matters.

Bare – bear

Bare offers no problem. As an adjective, it means 'naked, uncovered, very sparse'. As a verb it means 'to uncover'. For example:

> Her legs were bare. The travellers lived on the bare essentials. He bared his breast to the sword.

Bear, as a noun, refers to the wild animal. As a verb it means 'to carry'. For example:

> The porters will bear your supplies to the base camp.

The past tense is *bore* and the past participle is *borne*:

> They bore the supplies up the mountain.
> The supplies were borne by the porters.

So far so good; but a complication arises when *to bear* has the sense of giving birth. The past tense is *bore* (e.g. She bore him a son); the past participle is *born* (no final *e*!).

> The child was born two months ago.

However, *borne* is used as the past participle when it comes before *by* or after *have* and *had*. For example:

> Seven babies borne by Mrs Putnam died at birth.
> Mrs Proctor had borne two healthy children.

Break – brake

Brake is to do with reducing speed (past tense – *braked*).

   Break has the more general use of 'shattering, damaging, causing to fall apart' (past tense – *broke*).

Coarse – course

Coarse means 'rough, indelicate, vulgar', for example:

>   He had coarse hands. The cloth was of a coarse texture.

   Course is a word of wider application to do with moving along in a set direction:

>   The captain set course for Brazil.
>   He followed his college course with great success.
>   Your course of action will ruin the company.

Council – counsel

A *council* is a body of people who meet together to deliberate and take decisions. A member of such a body is a *councillor*. For example:

>   The District Council will consider applications for planning permission.
>   Elections to the Parish Council will take place in March.
>   After the dispute, three councillors resigned.

   Counsel means either 'advice', or (in the legal profession) one who gives such advice or one who pleads in court, usually a barrister. The word can also be used collectively for a group of barristers conducting a case. For example:

>   I would value your counsel on this problem.
>   The counsel for the defence argued effectively on the prisoner's behalf.

There is also a verb *to counsel*:

We must counsel you against doing anything in a hurry.

With the growth of organizations giving advice and support to people with problems, we are increasingly familiar with a phrase such as 'the counselling service'. A person who gives this service is a *counsellor*, as in:

> The teenager went to discuss her problems with the school counsellor.

Take care not to confuse the spellings of *councillor* and *counsellor*.

Creditable – credible – credulous

Creditable means 'deserving credit or praise', as in:

> The pianist gave a creditable performance of the *Moonlight Sonata*.

The other two words, *credible, credulous* (and their opposites *incredible* and *incredulous*) are all to do with 'believing'. Something which is very possible and hence easy to believe is said to be *credible*, as in:

> It is quite credible that one day life will be found on other planets.

Credulous is always applied to a person who believes things too readily and is therefore easy to deceive:

> People are remarkably credulous about what they read in the popular press.

Conversely, persons who find it difficult to believe something are said to be *incredulous*:

> Galileo found most people incredulous when he claimed that the earth went around the sun. To them it seemed incredible.

Currant – current

A *currant* is a small berry. *Current* refers to something on the move, running or flowing, whether it is sea-water, electricity or the affairs of the day as they flow past us:

> Current opinion in the UK is in favour of seat belts in cars.

Dependant – dependent

These two spellings distinguish between the noun and the adjective. A *dependant* (noun) is someone who depends on someone else for help or support, as in:

> The three dependants are her two young children and her aged father.

Dependent (adjective) describes someone or something relying on another:

> He was dependent on his mother until he was thirty.
> The dependent children were a source of worry to her.

Dessert – desert

Dessert is the sweet course of a meal.

Desert has a number of uses: (1) as a noun it means 'a sandy waste', as in:

> The camel train journeyed across the Sahara Desert.

The plural noun *deserts* means 'what one deserves', for example:

> The judge saw to it that he got his deserts.

(2) As a verb, *desert* is 'to abandon or to leave persons or places'. For example:

> The rogue deserted his wife and family.

It also has the special sense of abandoning one's duties in the armed forces without permission:

> Many soldiers deserted from the army after that battle.

Disinterested – uninterested

Both words may be used interchangeably to indicate a lack of interest in a subject, as in:

> The students were uninterested/disinterested in what the lecturer was telling them.

However, *disinterested* has a special meaning which is distinct from *uninterested* and it would be a pity if it were lost to common usage. *Disinterested* means 'impartial, unbiased'. Thus in a legal dispute the judge must always be disinterested but never uninterested! It would be as well for writers to maintain this useful distinction.

Draft – draught

In American usage the words are interchangeable, with the first spelling being the far more common. In Great Britain, *draft* is chiefly reserved for what is written – for example, a preliminary version of a speech or a literary composition; a banker's order.

It is also used in the armed services for a detachment sent on special duties, e.g. The draft from the first regiment embarked for India. Used as a verb, it means 'to send on such duties';

> Police were drafted into the area from other parts of the county.

The other meanings are conveyed by *draught* and include an unwelcome air current, swallowing a drink and the depth of a vessel in the water.

Emigrate – immigrate

The first word means 'to leave a country in order to live elsewhere' and the second means 'to enter an adopted country with the intention of living there'. Note the single m in *emigrate* and the double mm in *immigrate*.

Enormous – enormity

Some people regard enormity as the noun associated with enormous, meaning 'hugeness'. This is not so. The noun, little used though it is, is 'enormousness'. A quite different meaning is conveyed by enormity – 'an act of exceptional wickedness'. For example:

> The enormity of his crimes appalled the nation.

Both words convey something beyond what is normal: with enormous it is size; with enormity it is evil.

Flaunt – flout

These words are very often confused and misused.
To flaunt is 'to show off', often provocatively, as in:

> The family flaunted their new-found wealth in front of their neighbours.

To flout is 'to disregard accepted rules or laws', as in:

> By smuggling in his pet monkey, he outrageously flouted the rules of quarantine.

Forebear – forbear; foregoing – forgoing

The e makes all the difference!
Fore implies something that happened before and so a forebear is an ancestor and foregoing is something that occurred earlier. For example:

> In the foregoing chapter of my autobiography I told you how my forebears grew up in this city.

To forbear (without the e) is 'to refrain' or 'to hold back':

> I will forbear from saying what I really think of him.

To forgo is 'to relinquish' or 'to give up':

> As my mother is unwell, I must forgo the visit to the theatre.

Fortunate – fortuitous

These words are not interchangeable!

Fortunate of course means 'happy' or 'lucky'. *Fortuitous* means 'by chance'. For example:

> My meeting an old friend in a London street was quite fortuitous.

Hoard – horde

To *hoard* means 'to gather up and store away'. The noun refers to the store thus accumulated. For example:

> The citizens hoarded food as supplies ran short.
> Dragons were supposed to guard a hoard of gold.

Horde is a large disorganized group of persons or animals, as in:

> A horde of Christmas shoppers. A horde of wild buffalo.

Horrendous – horrid

The first word has become widely used in recent years as the strongest version of *horrid*, *horrible* and *horrific*. We might take this sequence as ascending degrees of awfulness. It is a pity we cannot fit in the obsolete word, *horrent*!

Illusion – delusion – allusion

The first two words refer to something which is not quite what it seems. An *illusion* is any misleading appearance and can apply to such things as conjuring tricks, a mirage in the desert or a false belief in one's own prospects! For example:

> The hope that she was about to give us a meal proved to be an illusion.

Delusion, while close in meaning, invariably conveys a suggestion of some error in a person's thinking or mental state:

He suffered from the delusion that the world would end at midnight.

Allusion is quite different from these and means 'a reference to something', as in:

The allusion to what the chairman said last week did not prove helpful.

Ingenious – ingenuous

Although very similar in appearance on the page, these words are quite unconnected in meaning. To be *ingenious* is to be clever and inventive. *Ingenuous* means 'frank, honest and sincere' – with the overtone of being somewhat simple-minded and not worldly-wise; naïve. For example:

When asked why she wanted the job, she made the ingenuous reply that she thought the uniform was pretty!

Disingenuous is not the opposite of *ingenuous* (which would be 'sophisticated'). It carries a sense of dishonesty, of being less than frank:

It is disingenuous for the developer to suggest that he wants this planning permission purely for the good of the community.

Lay – lie

These two distinct words cause endless confusion because the present tense of *lay* is the same as the past tense of *lie*. Think of them quite separately.

To lay, meaning 'to place something down', requires an object:

I now lay my plan before you. (present)
I will lay my cards on the table. (future)
She laid the flowers on his grave. (past)

This verb is used for birds laying eggs and people laying tables.

To lie requires no object. It conveys the meaning of being at rest in a horizontal position or just being situated (e.g. Ipswich lies to the east of London). The present tense is *lie*, the past tense is *lay* and the past participle is *lain*, as in:

> The ships lie in the harbour. (present)
> The wreckage lay on the beach. (past)
> It had lain there for days. (pluperfect)

When *to lie* means 'to tell an untruth', the situation is easier: e.g. Today he lies; yesterday he lied; some weeks ago he had lied.

Loathe – loath

Both these words derive from the same Anglo-Saxon source, meaning 'hateful'. But they have split apart, with *loathe* retaining the meaning of being filled with hatred or disgust. *Loath* (rhyming with '*both*') means 'reluctant, unwilling'.

Loose – lose

Loose (Rhyming with 'noose') is both an adjective and a verb. As an adjective it means 'unattached, not tight'. As a verb, it means 'to set free'. The past tense is *loosed*, as in:

> He loosed the rope and pushed the boat into the water.

Lose is a verb only, meaning 'to mislay something'. The past tense is *lost*. For example:

> I often lose things. Yesterday I lost a ring.

Morale – moral

Morale refers to the state of one's feelings or spirits:

> After three victories, the morale of the team was very high.

Moral is to do with an awareness of right and wrong. A moral person is one with a strict regard for doing what is right. An immoral person disregards the accepted codes of conduct. There is also a word *amoral*, which would be applied to a person who is unaware of the moral code or has completely rejected it. For example:

The first Director-General of the BBC was responsible for its high moral tone.

The immoral behaviour of famous people is featured prominently in the popular press.

The lost tribes of central America were happily amoral.

Personal – personnel

Whereas *personal* directs attention to an individual, *personnel* refers to a collection of people, such as a work-force or the crew of a ship. The term is well known in business and industry where the personnel manager deals with matters relating directly to the employees.

Practice – practise

As with 'licence' and 'license', the first word is a noun and the second a verb. For example:

We will be late for the tennis practice.
I must practise my back-hand more regularly.

Principle – principal

Principle is a noun meaning the natural law or cause on which something is based, as in:

It is best to study a subject from first principles.

Principal is an adjective meaning 'chief':

The principal advantage of this method is its cheapness.

The word is also used as a noun referring to the chief person in an organization. It is very common in educational establishments:

The principal of the college interviews all new students.

Stationary – stationery

'Standing still' is conveyed by *stationary*. The very similar word *stationery* means items to do with writing, such as notepaper, envelopes, pens, pencils, etc.

Their – there

A very common source of confusion, these two words are best learnt quite separately. *Their* is the possessive of *they*, and is used as in:

> The children ate their lunch at the table.
> I told jokes to my friends, much to their amusement.

It must not be confused with *there*, as in:

> There is a large house on the corner.
> I will phone you from the office as soon as I get there.

Weather – whether

Weather is used for climatic conditions, as in:

> We had a lot of sunny weather when we were on holiday.

Whether is used as an equivalent to 'if', as in:

> I wonder whether we shall meet again.

or added to the words 'or not' to express an alternative.

> You must do it, whether or not you want to.

Wright – write

A *wright* is a craftsman (e.g. wheelwright, shipwright). The chief victim of confusion between these two words is *playwright*. Because such a person *writes*, some people think his profession must be *playwrite*. This is quite wrong. The author of stage-plays is a craftsman – hence *playwright*.

Is it wrong?

Half-forgotten memories from school return to haunt us as we pause over a split infinitive, wonder about 'get' and 'got', and feel uneasy when we write 'hopefully'. Some things we were taught to avoid have now become an accepted part of the language. Some prohibitions had no secure basis in grammar anyway; others should still be observed. The following list offers advice on many of these problems:

Split infinitive

The infinitive part of the verb is introduced by *to*: e.g. to talk, to decide, to have seen, to have been visited. The old-established rule says 'never split an infinitive'. That is to say, do not insert a word between *to* and the rest of the infinitive in the following manner: to quietly talk, to beautifully dance, to bravely go, to really have seen.

Certainly these phrases are cumbersome, especially the last one, and they could easily be rearranged: to talk quietly, to dance beautifully, to go bravely, really to have seen.

All the same, there is no hard and fast rule against splitting an infinitive, despite what your teachers may have said. There is a danger in applying the rule unthinkingly, for it may create stilted phraseology such as, 'She decided partly to cook the meal before she went out.' Would it not be preferable to say, 'She decided to partly cook the meal before she went out'? As a writer, you will find a number of occasions when the most satisfactory way of expressing yourself includes a split infinitive.

However, you should take warning! So many people still shudder at the very idea of a split infinitive that it would be better to rephrase a doubtful sentence to avoid using one.

Ending a sentence with a preposition

The old schoolmaster's rule forbidding this is wrong. We frequently end sentences with prepositions and no harm is done:

e.g. I want to come in. The owner showed me around.

Suddenly the victim came to. Her behaviour is something I cannot put up with.

Different to

Writing early in the twentieth century, those great authorities, H. W. and F. G. Fowler in *The King's English* passed the opinion that 'different to' would come to replace 'different from' fairly soon. They have not been proved correct. 'Different to' is still frowned on. There is no grammatical reason why you should not use it but – as with the split infinitive – it is best to avoid giving offence to readers who think it is wrong.

Sometimes you may be tempted to say 'different than'. When followed by a noun or pronoun, this is incorrect:

> The new office is very different than our old one. (wrong)
> The new office is very different from our old one. (correct)

It *is* possible to use 'different than' if it is followed by a clause, as in:

> When you sing it is different than when you speak.

This is not incorrect, but it may upset your reader and it is easy enough to say, 'When you sing it is different from when you speak.' So stick to 'different from'.

Due to, owing to

The old rule says that *due* can only be used as an adjective: e.g. The fire was due to negligence. It is therefore incorrect to use it outside the clause as in this example:

> Due to negligence, the fire broke out. (wrong)

The phrase should be replaced by 'owing to' or 'because of', as in:

> Owing to negligence, the fire broke out.
> Because of negligence the fire broke out.

So much for the rule. Modern usage, however, frequently ignores this distinction and it seems only a matter of time before it ceases to matter. For the present, it might be as well to observe the rule.

Hopefully

A sentence such as: 'Hopefully my aunt will enjoy her visit', disturbs people who feel that the first word has stolen the place of 'I hope that . . .' They take the view that 'hopefully' should only be used to modify a verb, as in: 'We watched hopefully as the fireman climbed towards the boy.' Even so, the new use of 'hopefully' is so widespread that it can no longer be forbidden, but care should be taken that the meaning is absolutely plain. The following sentence leaves us in doubt: 'We will start tomorrow hopefully.' Does that mean 'we will start tomorrow full of hope' or does it mean 'we hope that we will start tomorrow'? Choose your words so that there is no doubt in the reader's mind.

He liked me talking to him

This is an example of the misuse of a gerund (a noun formed from a verb). The correct version is: 'He liked *my* talking to him.' Few of us would be careful enough to say this in ordinary conversation, but the rule should be observed in our writing. Let's take another example: 'The neighbour objected to him building a wall.' This is incorrect. The neighbour is not objecting to *him*; he is objecting to the building of a wall. We should therefore write, 'The neighbour objected to his building a wall.'

Got – get

High on the schoolmaster's list of forbidden words are 'get' and 'got'. They are not grammatically wrong but they easily become a habit. Once a writer allows himself to use 'got' instead of thinking of a more expressive word, the way is open to a whole succession of 'gots', as in this sentence: 'I got up, got my breakfast, got the early train and got to work by 8 o'clock.' You are unlikely to perpetrate anything as unpleasing as this, but it is surprising how often 'got' and 'get' will creep into your sentences unless you are on the alert.

Nice, terrible, awful, fantastic, great

This is a selection of words that have (or once had) a precise meaning. Now over-use has made them vague and inexpressive. A writer should consider carefully what feeling is to be conveyed and then seek the best words to express it. Do not be content with the first word that comes into your head. It may be one of these!

Shall — will

The rule says that a simple future is expressed as follows: I shall; he, she, it will; we shall; you will; they will: for example,

> I shall be in town tomorrow and you will then be able to see my new car.

Intention or determination to do something in the future is expressed by reversing the above in this way: I will; he, she, it shall; we will; you shall; they shall: for example,

> I will make every effort to help. They shall not interfere with your plans.

Common usage, however, is so varied that the best thing is to rely on what sounds right to you.

The reason is . . .

A common error is to combine two ways of giving a reason. It is incorrect to say 'the reason is because . . .'. Just say 'the reason is . . .'. For example:

> The reason they have come is the letter I sent.
> They have come because I sent the letter.

Between you and me

This is correct. Never say 'between you and I'.

Few — less

Generally speaking, 'few' should apply to numbers (e.g., There are very few people here today) and 'less' to quantity (e.g., I had less cake than she had.) However, 'less' is permissible with number if the number is thought of as a unified total. For example:

> The audience was just less than five hundred.
> *but* Fewer than five hundred people paid to see the show.

Other problems

Agreement

A source of many errors is the failure to make verbs agree with their subjects. A singular noun (or equivalent) must be followed by a singular verb (e.g., The man walks in the park) and a plural noun by a plural verb (e.g., The men walk in the park). In such easy sentences there is no problem, but here are five areas where you must be on your guard against errors of agreement:

1 *Either . . . or . . ./neither . . . nor . . .*
These offer alternatives and if each alternative is singular, then a singular verb is required. For example:

> Either the captain or the mate takes control of the ship.
> Neither the manager nor his assistant knows how to treat a customer.

When one alternative is singular and one is plural, the verb should agree with the alternative that is nearest, for example:

> Neither my sister nor my brothers live in the city.

2 *Each*
A singular verb follows 'each' if it is the subject of a sentence: for example,

> Each of the five secretaries has a telephone.

If 'each' comes after a plural noun or pronoun subject of the sentence, then the verb is plural:

e.g. The children were each given a toy.

3 Everyone, everybody

These words are singular and are therefore followed by singular verbs:

e.g. Everyone is happy to agree. Everybody understands this very well.

Similarly, 'no one', 'none', 'anyone', 'someone' take singular verbs.

e.g. No one in the room thinks she did it.

4 This kind of . . .

'Kind' is singular, but errors arise when the phrase continues with a plural noun which attracts (wrongly) a plural verb, as in:

This kind of men are always unlucky. (incorrect)
This kind of men is always unlucky. (correct)

The difficulty is removed and the sentence sounds better if we say, 'This kind of man is always unlucky.'

Beware of writing 'These kind of . . .' or 'These sort of . . .'. *These* and *those* should be followed by a plural noun (These kinds, those sorts).

5 Collective nouns

It is easy to say that a singular collective noun (e.g. company, audience, crowd) takes a singular verb. In practice, this is only appropriate when the group is regarded as one unit, as in:

The company takes its name from its founder.
An audience likes to be amused.
The flock of sheep is worth several thousand pounds.

If we see the group as a collection of individuals, then the plural is to be used after the collective noun, as in:

The flock of sheep are to be examined and then sheared.
The audience were divided in their reaction to the speaker.

The crew were delighted to go on shore leave.

Should 'number' be followed by a singular or plural word? The problem is neatly solved by Bill Bryson (*The Penguin Dictionary of Troublesome Words*, Penguin, 1987) who advises us always to follow 'the number' with a singular and 'a number' with a plural. For example:

> The number of travellers by air was five thousand.
> A number of travellers were air-sick.

Unrelated participle phrases

There is surely something wrong with these sentences:

> Walking around the house, the pillars came in view.
> Having scored a goal, the goal posts collapsed.
> Moving slowly, the mountain seemed more and more difficult.

The writer appears to be telling us of pillars which can walk around a house, goal posts that score goals and a mountain that moves slowly! He or she has overlooked the rule that a participle phrase (e.g. 'walking around the house') must relate to the noun next to it (e.g. 'the pillars'). These sentences should be rewritten. Possible versions would be:

> As they walked around the house, the visitors saw the pillars come into view.
> After he had scored a goal, the goal posts collapsed.
> Moving slowly, the climbers found the mountain more and more difficult.

Placing adverbs

The meaning of sentences may be changed if certain much-used adverbs are placed without due care. Think carefully where you should place 'only', 'even', 'also', 'just', 'mainly', 'nearly' and 'often'. A safe rule is to place these words beside the word or phrase to which they apply and not elsewhere in the sentence. See how the meaning changes with the placing of 'only' in these sentences:

Our only car salesman showed the prince the new model.
Our car salesman only showed the prince the new model.
Our car salesman showed only the prince the new model.
Our car salesman showed the only prince the new model.
Our car salesman showed the prince the only new model.
Our car salesman showed the prince the new model only.

Comparisons

Use 'like' before a noun or its equivalent; use 'as' before a verb. For example:

> She sang like an angel. They fought like animals. The wind howled like a demon in pain.
> *but:* He struggled as if he were mad. The soldiers behaved as their officers did.

(This is another of those rules to which exceptions may be found. No one could complain of 'The pedestrian felt *like* giving the motorist a piece of his mind.')

15 Handwriting

For your English to be truly clear, it has to be legible! In this age of typewriters and word processors this is not a problem in the business world but it certainly can be if your writing is done with a pen: this would apply to most students and to all of us who write personal letters and do not possess a typewriter. For certain kinds of writing a pen is actually preferable to a typewriter. A love letter, a letter of condolence, and even a routine 'thank you' letter convey more if the personality of the writer is stamped on them through the hand-writing – and handwriting is a very personal thing.

Unfortunately, this very quality can be an obstacle to communi-cation. People are as sensitive about their handwriting as they are about their speech: it is part of them and they resent attempts to persuade them to change. But a letter showing distinct personality may be very difficult to read. All of us must have come across hand-writing that is so small and cramped as to defy interpretation, while the flamboyant scrawl of another person may be only slightly more readable. Any suggestion that these kinds of handwriting might be improved is considered something of an insult and few of us would dare to suggest it to a friend or acquaintance.

Another defence of indifferent handwriting is 'I never could write very well' – with the unspoken implication '. . . and I don't intend to try now'. Yet with a quite small effort many poor writers could make a distinct improvement to their penmanship and win the heart-felt thanks of those of us who have to wrestle with their illegible scripts.

An improved handwriting can bring more material rewards too. In the world of education there is no doubt that, objective though they try to be, examiners are in a much better frame of mind when they mark a clearly written script than when they have to follow an argument which they can hardly decipher. The effort of trying to read the handwriting detracts from their concentration on the answer itself and, despite their efforts to be fair, their frustration can be reflected in the marks. (It is said that a group of examiners were once presented with the same set of essays twice over. On the first occasion they were handwritten. A few weeks later, when they had forgotten all about them, the very same set was presented to them for marking, but this time they were typed. The marks of the typed essays were significantly higher than for those that were handwritten.)

Employers often ask for letters of application to be handwritten, since they can assess something of a candidate's attitude from the handwriting. A legible script, neatly written and correctly laid out, makes an immediate good impression and suggests an applicant who would be a conscientious member of staff. On the other hand, badly written applications suggest that the candidates do not much care about getting the job and would be as casual in their attitude to work as they are in their letter writing. If you are not proud of your own handwriting, it might pay you to try and identify your particular weaknesses.

When we read, we do not spell out each letter to ourselves. We are accustomed to interpreting word-patterns with which we are familiar. You can easily read this page of print because the letters are clearly shaped and always the same and the word-patterns are consistent. You only study the individual letters if the word is very long and unfamiliar and you are trying to work it out. This principle applies to your handwriting. Are your letters clearly made and always consistent in their shape? It is easy to confuse small letters such as *o*, *e* and *a* if they are carelessly formed. An *e* which closes up its open shape can look like an *i*. A u with a closed-in top looks like an *a*.

Obscurity also comes from bad habits in joining – or not joining – letters together as you form them into words. Admittedly there are some styles of handwriting which do not join the letters but (as in print) rely on the clear and consistent placing of the letters. But most people have been brought up to join their letters and failure to do so properly is a source of difficulty. You should make sure that the tiny stroke joining one letter to the next does not alter the letter into something else. For example, if you join an *o* to another letter from the bottom rather than from the top, you may turn the *o* into an *a*. If you bring the join of an r downwards instead of across to the next letter, you turn it into an *n*.

An irritating fault is to join only some, but not all, of the letters within a single word. If the gap is more than very small indeed, the expected word-shape is broken and the eye hesitates in order to interpret it. Even in print it is disturbing to read 'convu lsion'; 'tradi tion'; 'untou chable'.

The expected word-shape is also destroyed if there is no clear differentiation between letters with stems above or below the line (e.g., b, d, f, g, h, j . . .) and those without stems (e.g., a, c, e, i, m . . .). Some writers reduce all the bigger letters to much the same size as the small ones and thereby render the word momentarily unrecognizable. *This is because the eye relies on the top half of the letters rather than the lower half.* You can test this at once by taking a piece of paper, covering the top half of a line of print and then trying to read it. You will find this quite difficult if you are unfamiliar with the text. Now cover the bottom half of a line and try again. You will find that you can read the text without any trouble at all. Therefore in your own handwriting make sure that the shape of your letters is especially clear in the top half and that stems on tall letters are seen clearly to rise above the lower portions of the letters. (Try to write the word 'rebellious' with all the letters the same size – stems included – and you will find the word almost unreadable.) Another habit which mars some people's handwriting is their use of capital letters instead of small ones. The letter S frequently tempts writers to this. It is so easy at the beginning of a word to give a quick swirl for this letter and the result is a misplaced capital. If it occurs in the middle of a word, the expected word-shape is ruined. The letter *f* is also a source of trouble if your basic training was a version of 'copper plate', because in that style *f* has an extension both above and below the line. Many writers reduce one or both of the extensions, once again upsetting what the eye expects.

The two most obvious features of anyone's hand are the size and the slope. Both are the expression of the writer's character and there can be no firm rule about them. However, a handwriting that is too small is hard on the eyes and too large a hand looks untidy and strange. As for slope, a slightly forward movement is the most agreeable. A pronounced backward slope looks awkward.

Finally check that you carefully dot your 'i's and cross your 't's. The tiny dots do help to sort out the 'i's from the misshaped 'e's and 'r's – provided of course that they are placed over the right letter!

There are several legible and attractive styles of handwriting. Perhaps the most beautiful script is italic, which requires special pens and much practice. Bad handwriting can often be traced to an imperfectly-learned style or one that is only half remembered and then modified by the user who mixes it with other styles to produce an unsatisfactory hybrid. Those who are left-handed have special problems which they solve in a variety of ways.

When all is said and done, you are judged by your handwriting, and if you are not pleased with it a few minutes' practice a day to overcome the faults you acknowledge in yourself could be well worth while.

Summary

Use this list to check your own weaknesses:

Are your letters well-shaped and clearly differentiated?
Are your letter-shapes consistent?
Is your method of joining letters satisfactory?
Do you make unnecessary breaks in the middle of words?
Are the letters with stems clearly differentiated in height and depth from those without stems?
Are you using some capital letters instead of small ones?
Check on how you form s and f.
Is the slope of your handwriting acceptable?
Is your writing too small or too large?
Are you careful about dotting the is and crossing the ts?

16 Clear Speech

By far the most common form of English communication you will engage in is not written at all. It is *speech*. You should not be surprised to find a book on 'Clear English' with a section on the spoken language because nowadays the importance of Spoken English is widely recognized. It is a compulsory part of the GCSE examination for sixteen-year-olds, who cannot receive a certificate for English unless they satisfy the examiners in their oral work. Employers rate it highly, not only for important managerial posts but also for the many other jobs where employees have contact with the public in shops and offices.

Our social life is also enhanced if we have confidence in our own ability to speak to people and express ourselves clearly. One has only to think of the unhappiness and even tragedies that have been caused in human relationships by a lack of communication between people, especially within families with the young unable to speak to the old and vice versa. Of course this kind of communication problem has deep roots in personal emotions and the fear and tensions that have built up over the years and no handbook on 'Clear English' can attempt to tackle that. But it does remind us how important our spoken communication is and the value of being able to express ourselves adequately when we have to talk to other people.

Let us consider some professional and social occasions when clear English will mean clear spoken English. Of great importance to so many people (older as well as younger) is the job interview. The letter of application and the CV will be set out in writing, but what decides whether or not you get the job is the impression you make at the interview – and this is a spoken encounter.

Once you have obtained the job, the ability to speak acceptable English will often be a factor in the race for promotion. Managers of firms are very concerned about their public image and employees who by their speech and manner can convey a good impression of the firm and its products or services will be preferred to those who are inarticulate.

The higher one goes in an organization the more occasions there will be for talking to people. It may be negotiating one-to-one; it will almost certainly involve addressing groups of people. This is known as 'giving a presentation'. When you do this, you will not only be talking to an audience but also showing videos, demonstrating products, explaining charts and so on. The person who can hold the attention of a room full of fellow professionals and handle their probing questions is an invaluable member of the firm.

In one's social life, the chance to talk to groups of people can arise in all sorts of ways. There are local community meetings, parish councils, social clubs, charity organizations and school associations. All these welcome the person who can state a case or put a point of view clearly and agreeably. Once you are proved to be an effective speaker, honorary posts come your way and you find yourself approached to be the chairman, secretary or committee member of organizations in which you have shown interest. You will then find that the ability to read aloud is an advantage, for chairmen have to read reports and secretaries begin meetings by reading aloud the minutes of the previous session. A good speaker is not necessarily a good reader, yet both arts can be cultivated with advantage if some kind of public office is thrust upon you.

A full treatment of this whole subject is to be found in the author's *Public Speaking* (Penguin, 1988). For the moment, we can offer some advice under the headings of 'What to Say' and 'How to Say It'.

What to say . . .

The first thing is to know what you want to say before you try to say it! This differs from the act of writing where, as we have seen, you often discover your meaning and order your thoughts by the very means of writing your first draft. You cannot do this when you make a speech. Imagine the chaos if a speaker got to his feet and began thinking aloud, gradually fighting towards the message through the jumble of ideas in his mind! We all have suffered from extempore speakers who like the sound of their own voices but have no real idea of what they are talking about. To be effective, decide in advance exactly what points you want to put over. It will help if you write them down. Once again, the act of writing helps to clarify your thoughts and render them coherent.

Once you know what you are trying to say, decide the best order for your points and write them down accordingly. This will give you an outline of your speech. The next thing to do is to write it out. Very experienced speakers can forgo this stage in the process; they will be able to improvise their speeches guided only by the list of headings. For the less experienced, drafting out the speech in writing is very advisable. It enables you to find the words necessary to flesh out the bare bones of headings; it gives you time to think of illustrations and examples, and it enables you to work out the words which are going to lead you from one point to the next.

As you write the speech, think in *spoken* English and not in written English. There is a marked difference between the two modes and you do not want your speech to sound like a spoken essay. Therefore imagine yourself saying the speech as you write it. This will produce the vocabulary and turns of phrase that would be used by you as a speaker and not as a writer. You will find that quite naturally you are using abbreviations (aren't, won't) and colloquial expressions because this is how people speak. Your sentences will fall into comfortable speech patterns and will not be moulded for their literary effect. Above all, it will be your own voice that is going down on paper as an intermediate step towards the time when your voice will be speaking the words to an audience.

After you have written the first draft of your speech, give special attention to the way you are going to begin and end it. Often it pays to draft out the main body of the speech before you plan the opening. Then, when you know the shape of your remarks, you can devise an opening that will catch the audience's attention. There are several ways of doing this and much depends on the tone and subject matter of your speech. If your intention is to amuse, then a funny story will set the mood; if the subject is more serious, then a striking fact or statistic to concentrate the minds of the audience would be more appropriate. In many circumstances some kind of anecdote involving people (and especially the speaker himself) compels attention.

The conclusion to a talk should also be carefully planned. You want to leave the audience with a firm impression of what you have been trying to put over to them. Do not weary them with a long 'recap' of all you have said. Choose the most important point and build your speech towards this and then leave your audience with a well-phrased remark that will fix the point in their minds and which also clearly signals that the speech is over.

With a good opening and a satisfying conclusion built into your first draft, you can now read over the whole speech to see how it goes. There is something to be said for reading it silently and quite rapidly at first. This will enable you to gauge the shape and balance of the speech. Perhaps a point is taking up too much time or an illustration is needed to make a certain argument more effective. You may find some expressions which seem awkward and require rephrasing.

Once you have sorted out these problems and thereby produced a second draft of the speech, you can try reading it aloud. Putting the words on your tongue is the real test and, as a result, you may want to make further changes. Things that look right do not always sound right!

How to say it . . .

Once you are satisfied that you have achieved on paper the best you can do, you now have to prepare yourself for delivering the speech to an audience. There is one golden rule: *you must not read your speech.* The script you have written is a stage in the preparation and a most important one. Now you must be brave enough to leave it behind. How is this to be done? Certainly not by memorizing the speech verbatim. This would be almost as bad as reading aloud and would produce an equally unnatural result. What is more, your memory might let you down and leave you groping for words in front of the audience.

A useful technique is as follows: read your text to yourself three or four times so that you become thoroughly familiar with what you want to say, but not so familiar that you begin to memorize it parrot-fashion. As you study the speech, underline the key point in each section (or highlight it with a coloured glow-pen). Allow yourself to memorize these sentences only. The result should be that you can recall confidently the outline of your talk, moving from one key point to the next, and having in your mind the supporting material which you yourself have drafted. To give you confidence and to prompt you when you are on your feet, you can prepare notes to hold in your hand. The best form of these is the set of notecards, postcard size or a little smaller. On these you can write cue phrases to remind you of each main point in turn. Resist the temptation to fill the notecards with long sentences (you won't have time to read them) and do not try, as some have done, to write the whole speech in microscopic handwriting! Instead, be courageous and write very boldly just two or three cue phrases on each card – and not more. If you have prepared your speech thoughtfully and rehearsed it sensibly, using only the notes on the cards, then you will find yourself speaking directly to the audience in words that, although closely related to what you originally drafted, are coming freshly from you as real speech and will vary when you deliver the speech another time and to another audience.

Using your voice

Bad handwriting is a small obstacle to written communication these days when typewriters and word processors are readily available. But the best speech will count for nothing if the voice of the speaker is inaudible. A poor delivery will also mar one's chances in an interview. Most people have voices serviceable enough for all their daily speech activities: it is on those special occasions when you have to address a whole group of people or hold your own in important negotiations that many of us lose confidence, or do all we can to avoid the challenge.

It would take much more space than is available in this short section to consider in detail what makes a good voice and how it can be cultivated, but here are some suggestions to help you if faced with the necessity of speaking in public or making a good impression in an interview:

1 Take a good breath before you speak. Shallow breathing produces a shallow tone. What is more, a good deep breath brings confidence and steadies the nerves.

2 Be prepared to move your lips, tongue and jaw more

vigorously than usual. Too often we rely on indeterminate mouth shapes and so produce indeterminate sounds. Firm consonants and well-shaped vowels give a satisfying clarity to one's speech.

3 Adopt a good stance. A speaker who droops over his or her notes and keeps the head down is unlikely to be heard very far down the hall. In an interview, do not slump in your chair. Look alert and you are more likely to sound alert. If you are reading aloud (say, the minutes of a meeting), hold the book up, though not so high as to obscure your face.

4 Speak a little more slowly and articulate more clearly than you would in ordinary conversation.

5 Make sure your voice is loud enough when you address a group. Always have in mind the listeners at the back of the audience and make sure they can hear you. Guard against the tendency of many speakers to drop their voices as they go on. From time to time reassert the volume level at which you began.

6 Consider the pitch of your voice. Nerves make some speakers become shrill, while others let their voices drop away to a low-pitched mumble. Ask a good friend for an opinion of your voice. It is very probable that you will need to raise the pitch for it to carry in a large room.

7 Accept your natural accent and don't feel self-conscious about it. The important thing is to speak English clearly, with interest and vigour, with whatever accent is natural to you. A regional accent, well spoken and clearly articulated, has much more personality than an adopted Standard English accent in which the speaker does not feel at home. The test is *communication*. Only if your accent is a barrier to communication should it cause you concern.

Interviews

A kind of spoken English quite different from that used in addressing meetings is required for an interview. Whereas a presentation is a set piece, capable of rehearsal, an interview is by its very nature impromptu. But this does not mean that it has to be totally unprepared. If you have to undergo an interview – whether it be for a job or to sell an idea or to get something you want from officialdom – then time spent on preparation is time well spent. Work out in advance the points you want to make in the interview or the information you wish to find out. Put yourself in the place of the interviewer and think of all the things that he or she may ask you and prepare possible answers to them. It is not just a matter of having the information in your head; you need the words as well. The interviewer will be impressed if you express yourself in clear English and you are more likely to do this if you have gone over possible questions and answers beforehand and have actually put them into words. You may want to try these over in the privacy of your bedroom, but it would be far more useful if a good friend would ask you the questions, challenging you to find the words for your answer. With this kind of preparation behind you, the chances of your mumbling and stumbling in front of the interviewer will be much reduced. An interview appears to be a spontaneous exchange, but you have everything to gain by making preparations in advance.

This subject is treated fully in the author's *Public Speaking* (Penguin Self-Starter 1988).

FOR THE BEST IN PAPERBACKS, LOOK FOR THE

In every corner of the world, on every subject under the sun, Penguin represents quality and variety – the very best in publishing today.

For complete information about books available from Penguin – including Puffins, Penguin Classics and Arkana – and how to order them, write to us at the appropriate address below. Please note that for copyright reasons the selection of books varies from country to country.

In the United Kingdom: Please write to *Dept E.P., Penguin Books Ltd, Harmondsworth, Middlesex, UB7 0DA.*

If you have any difficulty in obtaining a title, please send your order with the correct money, plus ten per cent for postage and packaging, to *PO Box No 11, West Drayton, Middlesex*

In the United States: Please write to *Dept BA, Penguin, 299 Murray Hill Parkway, East Rutherford, New Jersey 07073*

In Canada: Please write to *Penguin Books Canada Ltd, 2801 John Street, Markham, Ontario L3R 1B4*

In Australia: Please write to the *Marketing Department, Penguin Books Australia Ltd, P.O. Box 257, Ringwood, Victoria 3134*

In New Zealand: Please write to the *Marketing Department, Penguin Books (NZ) Ltd, Private Bag, Takapuna, Auckland 9*

In India: Please write to *Penguin Overseas Ltd, 706 Eros Apartments, 56 Nehru Place, New Delhi, 110019*

In the Netherlands: Please write to *Penguin Books Netherlands B.V., Postbus 195, NL–1380AD Weesp*

In West Germany: Please write to *Penguin Books Ltd, Friedrichstrasse 10–12, D–6000 Frankfurt/Main 1*

In Spain: Please write to *Longman Penguin España, Calle San Nicolas 15, E–28013 Madrid*

In Italy: Please write to *Penguin Italia s.r.l., Via Como 4, I-20096 Pioltello (Milano)*

In France: Please write to *Penguin Books Ltd, 39 Rue de Montmorency, F-75003 Paris*

In Japan: Please write to *Longman Penguin Japan Co Ltd, Yamaguchi Building, 2–12–9 Kanda Jimbocho, Chiyoda-Ku, Tokyo 101*